RP.

THE Heinemann *English* PROGRAMME 2

John Seely   *David Kitchen*

With Special Projects by

Frank Green and Christopher Stubbs

D1103222

Heinemann

Heinemann Educational
a division of Heinemann Publishers (Oxford) Ltd,
Halley Court, Jordan Hill, Oxford OX2 8EJ

OXFORD   LONDON   EDINBURGH
MADRID   ATHENS   BOLOGNA   PARIS
MELBOURNE   SYDNEY   AUCKLAND   SINGAPORE   TOKYO
IBADAN   NAIROBI   HARARE   GABORONE
PORTSMOUTH NH (USA)

First published 1995

98 97 96 95
10 9 8 7 6 5 4 3 2 1

British Library Cataloguing in Publication data
for this title available from the British Library.

ISBN 0 435 10354 7

Designed and produced by Gecko Limited, Bicester, Oxon

Printed in Spain by Mateu Cromo

Acknowledgements

We would like to thank the following for permission to reproduce
copyright material:

Books for Keeps for 'A Visit to Berlie's' No. 76 (Sept 1992); Felicity
Bryan for 'I Hate the Snake' by Richard Edwards; Consumers'
Association for 'Will next year see trainers...' and 'It's a bargain ... or
is it' from *Check it Out!* (Dec/Jan 1992/1993); *Daily Express* for
'High rise clamper' (3 Jan 1992); Faber and Faber for 'Icarus' by
Judith Nicholls from *Dragonsfire and other Poems*; Hamish Hamilton
Ltd for 'Listn Big Brodda Dread, Na' by James Berry from *When I
Dance* © James Berry 1988 first published by Hamish Hamilton
Children's Books; Harper Collins Publishers Ltd for 'Horror Film' from
Song of the City by Gareth Owen; *The Independent* for 'Guide to a
happy Christmas' first published in *The Indy* (20 Dec 1993), for
'Indignation and tears down among the ferrets' (3 Jan 1994), for 'The
Last daredevils use kites to rocket' by James Kanter (13 Sept 1993),
for 'Car clamper rises to new heights'; Molly Weir for an extract from
Shoes were for Sunday (1973); Leslie Norris for 'Boy Flying' from
The Kingfisher Book of Children's Poetry (1985); Oxford University
Press for 'The Prodigal Son' from *Junk Mail* by Michael Harrison
(1993) © Michael Harrison; Penguin Books for 'When Mrs Hopkins ...'
by Susan Gregory from *Martini-on-the Rocks* © Susan Gregory 1984
first published by Viking Children's Books; Random House UK Ltd for
an extract from *The TV Kid* by Betsy Byars published by The Bodley
Head; Reed Consumer Books for 'A Snake in the Grass' by R K
Narayan from *Under the Banyan Tree* published by William
Heinemann Ltd, for an extract from *Granny Was A Buffer Girl* by
Berlie Doherty published by Methuen Children's Books; Walker Books
Limited for an extract from *The Country Boy* by Bernard Ashley ©
Bernard Ashley 1989, for an extract from *Badger on the Barge* by
Janni Howker © Janni Howker 1984.

Every effort has been made to contact copyright holders. We would be
glad to rectify any omissions at the next reprint if notice is given to the
publisher.

We would like to thank the following for permission to reproduce
photographs on the pages noted:

J. Allan Cash Ltd: p82 (glassblower), p83 (trekking, market stall);
Comstock Photo Library: p131 (canal with theatre); Barnaby's Picture
Library: p27, p67; Jon Davison/Berlitz Publishers: p82 (Caves of Arta),
p83 (Aquapark at Magaluf); Sarah Fenwick: p161; Robert Harding
Picture Library: p84, p137 (interior of bedroom, beach); Chris
Honeywell: p23, p37, pp62–63, p137 (chocolates, money, Levis,
electronic keyboard, Sega Game Gear, leather jacket), pp153–157;
NHPA/Stephen Dalton: p7 (snake), p127 (lizard); Oxford Scientific
Films: p127 (praying mantis); Philip Parkhouse: p137 (satellite dish);
Popperfoto: p27 (cotton mill, changing bobbins, hop pickers), p67;
Rex Features: p114; John Seely: p25, p129–130, p131 (Stratford canal
– bridge), p132; Sony UK Ltd: p137 (Sony diskman, CD stacking
system); Spectrum Colour Library: p82 (Marineland in Mallorca), p83
(fishing); Zefa: p82 (Bellver Castle).

Introduction

The Heinemann English Programme Book 2 offers a range of lively, enjoyable materials to help you develop your abilities in reading, writing, and speaking and listening.

Each unit contains a rich mix of fiction (stories, poems, playscripts), non-fiction (autobiography, information writing, newspapers, magazine articles) and activities based on a theme.

In each unit you will also find activities to develop your knowledge of and skills in **Language Study**. You will learn best about spelling, grammar and punctuation when these things are related to your own reading, writing and speaking and listening. That is why the language activities in this book are all part of thematic units.

The **Special Projects** offer opportunities to work in groups, solve problems together and develop your skills in reading and writing in a variety of forms.

The Heinemann English Programme will help you to assess your own work so you can see how you are progressing in English. The grids at the beginning of each unit explain what you do and why you do it. In the Teacher's File which accompanies this book you will find student self-assessment sheets with guidance on assessing your work.

The Teacher's File also contains details of curriculum coverage for each unit, information about Language Study, a guide to the differentiation strategy in *The Heinemann English Programme*, photocopiable support and extension sheets, drama activities and assessment guidance.

We hope you find all *The Heinemann English Programme* has to offer interesting, useful and, above all, enjoyable.

Key to symbols in this book

| TF | There is an extension or support worksheet for this activity available in the Teacher's File. |

| EXT | This is an extension piece suitable for more able students. |

Contents

I hate the snake!

Page	Title	What you do	Why you do it
7	**I hate the snake!**	Think about words to describe snakes. In a group write all your ideas down. Share all your ideas with the rest of the class.	To share ideas. To develop your vocabulary. To start you thinking about the theme of the unit.
8–9	**The snake**	Read the poem and answer questions about it. Look at the poet's descriptive words about the snake's movement.	To develop your skills as a reader. To develop your vocabulary.
10	**'Hissiness'?**	Make up words that end in -ness. Look at how words are made and write as many words as you can that start in the same way.	To learn about how words are made, and to learn about suffixes.
11	**Following the pattern**	Write a poem following a similar pattern to 'The snake'.	To write a poem using your own ideas following a simple pattern.
12–14	**Richard Edwards' snakes**	Look at the pages of information on snakes. Look at the different ways the information is given. Draw up a table and use it to record the information on four snakes. Write a short text for primary school children.	To learn how to present information in different ways for different audiences and purposes.
15	**In brief**	Study how to write in brief.	Learn how to write information in brief, without missing out anything important.
16	**When to use capital letters**	Read the information on capital letters and correct the text at the bottom of the page.	To develop your skills as a writer and learn how and when to use capital letters.
17–20	**A snake in the grass**	Read the story and answer the questions as you go. Then sort out what you learnt about each character. Think about the story from different points of view and imagine the setting. Make up your own story that is started for you.	To develop close reading skills. To develop your skills as a writer.
21	**It sounds like 'a'**	List words that contain an 'a' sound. Do a word puzzle based on the names of snakes found earlier on in the unit.	To improve your spelling. To develop your vocabulary.

I hate the snake!

Do you?
Some people shrivel up at the very thought.
Some people faint if they just see one.
Others think they are 'really, really int'resting'.
There are quite a lot of snakes in this chapter.
Some poisonous...
    some harmless...
        and some which may not even exist.

Let's start with some words...

...words to describe the thoughts and feelings
you have when you see a snake like this one.

On your own

Take a piece of paper and write down:

- all the words that come into your head when you look at
  the snake on this page
- the words that come into your head when you think about
  snakes in general
- any other words you could use to describe this snake.

In a group

Brainstorm 'snake words':

- choose someone to write all the ideas down on a sheet of paper
- everyone in the group says any words they can think of that the
  picture, or the word 'snake' suggests to them
- no comments
- no criticisms.

Just see how many you can think of.

Then share

Share your ideas with the rest of the class and see how
many different words the whole class has thought of.

The snake

I hate the snake
I hate the snake
I hate the way it trails and writhes
And slithers on its belly in the dirty dirt and creeps
I hate the snake
I hate its beady eye that never sleeps.

I love the snake
I love the snake
I love the way it pours and glides
10 And essses through the desert and loops necklaces on trees
I love the snake
Its zigs and zags, its ins and outs, its ease.

I hate the snake
I hate the snake
I hate its flickering liquorice tongue
Its hide and sneak, its hissiness, its picnic-wrecking
I hate its yawn
Its needle fangs, their glitter and their bite.

I love the snake
20 I love the snake
I love its coiled elastic names
Just listen to them: hamadryad, bandy-bandy,
Sidewinder, asp
And moccasin and fer de lance and adder

And cascabel
And copperhead
Green mamba, coachwhip, indigo,
So keep your fluffy kittens and your puppy-dogs,
I'll take
30 The boomslang and
The anaconda. Oh, I love the snake!

Richard Edwards

The poem begins 'I hate the snake', and ends with the words
'Oh, I love the snake!' In between, the writer gives us all sorts
of reasons on both sides. Look through the poem again.

1 Find the strongest reason for loving the snake.
2 Explain why.
3 Find the strongest reason for hating the snake.
4 Explain why.

Different sides of the argument

Look carefully at the first two verses of the poem.
Compare the middle lines of each:

I hate the way it trails and writhes
And slithers on its belly in the dirty dirt and creeps

I love the way it pours and glides
And esses through the desert and loops necklaces on trees

5 In what ways are they similar?
6 Why are they different?
7 Do you think the poet does this on purpose? If so, why?

The poet's words

One of the things that makes this a good poem to read aloud is
the poet's choice of words.

8 Find two words that describe the snake's movement and say
   why you think they are effective.
9 Find two words or groups of words that describe the shapes
   the snake makes. Do these give a good picture of a snake?
10 The poem ends in a celebration of the variety of strange
   names given to snakes. Choose two that you like the sound
   of and explain why.

'Hissiness'?

If you look up 'hissiness' in the dictionary, you won't find it. Richard Edwards has made it up. Even so, you probably didn't find it hard to understand. This is because he has followed a pattern for making nouns.

1 What other words can you think of ending in **-ness**? Make a list of them.
2 Look at the words in your list – can you work out which words they have been made from?
3 What word has 'hissiness' been made from? (And what has *that* been made from?)

New words from old

Nouns can be made from verbs, adjectives, and other nouns. This is done by adding another part, a **suffix**, to the end of the word.

word	+	suffix	=	new word
teach	+	er	=	teacher

verb	→	noun	adjective	→	noun
teach		teach**er**	happy		happ**iness**
amaze		amaz**ement**	stupid		stupid**ity**

Any more?

1 Write each of the four suffixes from the table above at the top of a column.
2 Under each one, write as many words as you can think of that end with that suffix.

Following the pattern

Richard Edwards' poem makes a good pattern for writing poems of your own.

Two routes

- If you want to, you can go straight ahead and copy those parts of the poem's pattern that you like. Just choose an interesting subject and start writing.
- If you would like more guidance, follow the arrows – but remember – as soon as you are ready to write, just start writing.

Think of a subject

Try to think of something that people can both love and hate.

Think of an argument

- Make a list of all the reasons why people might love this subject.
- Make a second list of why people might hate it.

Look at the pattern

Make up some sentences that start like this:

I hate its
I hate the way it
I love its
I love the way it

Build the argument

- Think about how the argument might go.
  Who wins, and why?
  (In 'The snake' it is the *names* that lead the writer to decide that he loves snakes.)
- Look at the sentences you have written. Select those that fit the argument best and sort them into a good order.
- Write out your sentences in the order you have chosen.

Build the poem

Now forget about the notes you have made and just look at the list of sentences you have written out. Ask yourself, 'What is missing?'
Add sentences and ideas that build up the poem. Try to imagine it as a conversation between two voices.

Richard Edwards' snakes

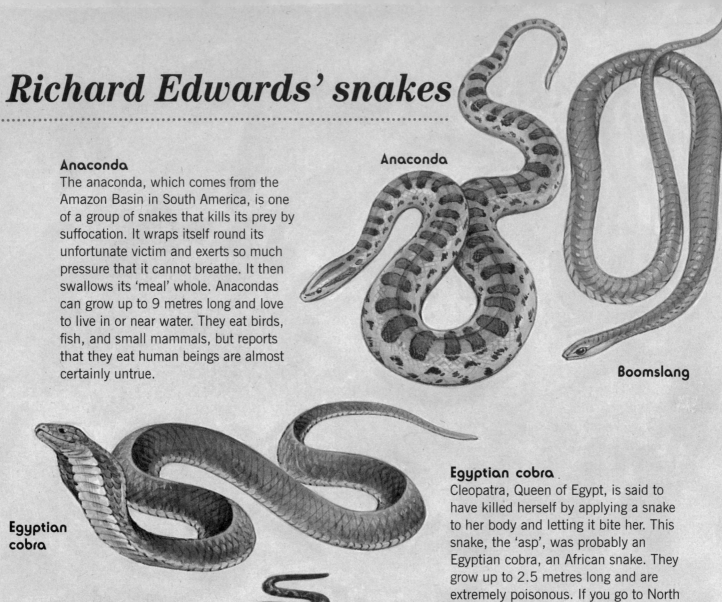

Anaconda

The anaconda, which comes from the Amazon Basin in South America, is one of a group of snakes that kills its prey by suffocation. It wraps itself round its unfortunate victim and exerts so much pressure that it cannot breathe. It then swallows its 'meal' whole. Anacondas can grow up to 9 metres long and love to live in or near water. They eat birds, fish, and small mammals, but reports that they eat human beings are almost certainly untrue.

Anaconda

Boomslang

Egyptian cobra

Cleopatra, Queen of Egypt, is said to have killed herself by applying a snake to her body and letting it bite her. This snake, the 'asp', was probably an Egyptian cobra, an African snake. They grow up to 2.5 metres long and are extremely poisonous. If you go to North Africa on holiday and see a snake charmer, the snake he uses is very likely to be an Egyptian cobra.

Egyptian cobra

Terciopello

Terciopello

This is a large pit viper (see panel) which lives in Central America, where it is probably the commonest poisonous snake. It has a number of local names, including: fer de lance, yellow jaw, tommygoff and barba amarilla.

I hate the snake!

Copperhead

Cascabel, or neotropical rattlesnake

This species of rattlesnake lives in Central and South America, from Mexico to Argentina. It grows up to 1.8 metres in length. It is poisonous, and very dangerous, because its venom attacks not only the blood system, but also the nervous system.

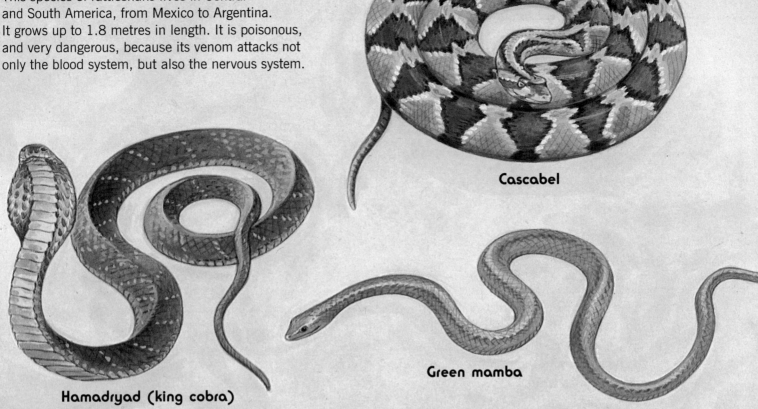

Cascabel

Green mamba

Hamadryad (king cobra)

Sidewinding

Snakes move in a number of different ways. Those that live in sandy deserts and other places where there is little on the ground for their skin to grip on have developed a method of moving called sidewinding. The snake raises its head and pushes it to one side. As it touches the ground again, the rest of the body is pulled across to follow in a kind of half 'jump'. In this way the snake makes a series of steps at forty-five degrees to the angle of its body.

Pit vipers

A large group of snakes that have an area close to the eye which is very sensitive to changes in temperature (pit organ). Vipers can detect a change in temperature of as little as $\frac{1}{3000}$ degree Celsius. This enables them to hunt their warm-blooded prey even when it is completely dark.

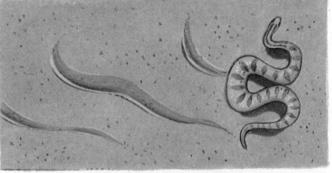

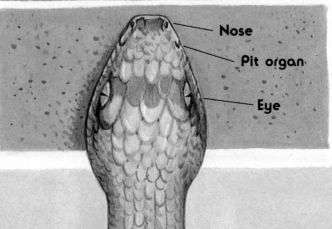

Nose

Pit organ

Eye

Presenting information

The pages of an information book, like pages 12–13, present us with information in a variety of forms:

- illustrations
- captions
- diagrams
- text.

The text may be in full sentences, as it is on those two pages. It may also be in brief, like the table below.

Compare these two kinds of text. What do you think are the advantages and disadvantages of each?

Try it out

TF

1 Making a table

- Draw up a table like the one below.
- Use it to record the information about the four snakes described on pages 12–13.
- If you are not sure how to fill in the *Other information* column, look at the section opposite: **In brief**.

2 Writing it up

- Imagine that you have been asked to write the text for a picture book about snakes for primary school children.
- It is to be based on the information in the table below.
- The sentences must be clear and easy to understand.
- Choose two of the snakes from the table below and write the text for each one.

NAME	REGION	SIZE	POISONOUS?	APPEARANCE	OTHER INFORMATION
boomslang	S. Africa	up to 1.85m	very	thin, brown (female), variable (male)	lives in trees, difficult to see, can move fast, can swim, when frightened blows itself up to several times normal size
copperhead	N. America	60–90 cm	yes	orange or copper colour, with red-brown bands	pit viper, bite painful, but not usually fatal to humans
green mamba	Africa	2m+	very	green	lives in trees, moves fast, bite can be fatal to humans (attacks blood and nervous systems)
king cobra	India	up to 5.5m	yes	thin, olive-green or brown with bronze eyes	eats other snakes, takes great care of young, bite rarely fatal to humans, also known as **hamadryad**

In brief

When we are writing something for other people to read we normally write in full sentences. Sometimes, however, we want to present information as *briefly* as possible:

How brief?

The problem is that if you make your message too brief, other people may not understand. So the rules are:

- be as brief as possible
- don't miss out vital information
- when you have written it, read it as if you were the person you are writing for. Ask yourself, 'Will they find it confusing?'

Which words can be missed out?

Compare these two versions:

It **lives in trees**, and can **move fast**. Its **bite can be fatal to human** beings because it **attacks** both the **blood** system **and** the **nervous system**.

Lives in trees, moves fast, bite can be fatal to humans (attacks blood and nervous systems).

green mamba, or Green Mamba –
when do you use capital letters?

You use a capital letter for:

the beginning of a sentence, or a new piece of direct speech	**He** seemed unhappy, just muttering, '**G**ood morning,' as he sidled past.
the personal pronoun 'I'	'Actually, **I** don't want to talk to you,' he said.
people's initials and abbreviations that are made up from the first letters of words	**A.B.** Carter **USA** = United States of America
the first letters of titles of people and organisations	**M**rs Thatcher, the former **P**rime **M**inister the **C**ounty **C**ouncil
the first letter of proper nouns: ■ people's names ■ place names ■ names of days and months.	**J**ennifer **H**arries **T**hailand, **N**ether **W**allop **T**uesday, **D**ecember
One problem is caused by titles of television programmes, plays, films, books: ■ some people use capitals for all the words ■ some people use capitals for the main words ■ some people use capitals for just the first word. **The important thing is to choose one of these and stick to it.**	**T**he **T**aming **O**f **T**he **S**hrew **T**he **T**aming of the **S**hrew **T**he taming of the shrew
Important Capitals are not normally used for the names of plants, animals, or birds.	green mamba

Capitals, please

Where should there be capital letters in this text?

will next year see trainers worn for sport and not as street cred fashion accessories? according to dawn clover at the british shoe corporation: 'trainers have died out quite a bit. in 1993, they won't have a place in the high fashion marketplace.' but for sporty types, trainer manufacturers promise more special features to help your performance in 1993.

■ puma have updated the disc system.
■ adidas have introduced a shock-absorbing material called dynaprene.
■ reebok's top-of-the-range models will include a co2 gas cylinder!
■ nike's 'blow-moulded' technology will turn air nike into 'air max'.

A snake in the grass

On a sunny afternoon, when the inmates of the bungalow were at their siesta, a cyclist rang his bell at the gate frantically and announced: 'A big cobra has got into your compound. It crossed my wheel.' He pointed to its track under the gate, and resumed his journey.

The family consisting of the mother and her four sons assembled at the gate in great agitation. The old servant, Dasa, was sleeping in the shed. They shook him out of his sleep and announced to him the arrival of the cobra. 'There is no cobra,' he replied and tried to
10 dismiss the matter. They swore at him and forced him to take an interest in the cobra. 'The thing is somewhere here. If it is not found before the evening, we will dismiss you. Your neglect of the garden and the lawns is responsible for all these dreadful things coming in.' Some neighbours dropped in. They looked accusingly at Dasa: 'You have the laziest servant on earth,' they said. 'He ought to keep the surroundings tidy.' 'I have been asking for a grass-cutter for months,' Dasa said. In one voice they ordered him to manage with the available things and learn not to make demands. He persisted. They began to speculate how much it would cost to buy a
20 grass-cutter. A neighbour declared that you could not think of buying any article made of iron till after the war. He chanted banalities of wartime prices. The second son of the house asserted that he could get anything he wanted at controlled prices. The neighbour became eloquent about the black market. A heated debate followed. The rest watched in apathy.

Questions

1 How many people have we met so far?
2 What have we learned about each one?
3 What picture have you formed of the family and its life?
4 What do you think will happen next?

The Heinemann English Programme 2

At this point the college boy of the house butted in with: 'I read in an American paper that 30,000 people die of snake bite every year.' Mother threw up her arms in horror and arraigned Dasa. The boy elaborated the statistics. 'I have worked it out, 83 a day. That means every twenty minutes someone is dying of cobra bite. As we have been talking here, one person has lost his life somewhere.' Mother nearly screamed on hearing it. The compound looked sinister. The boys brought in bamboo sticks and pressed one into the hands of the servant also. He kept desultorily poking it into the foliage with a cynical air. 'The fellow is beating about the bush,' someone cried aptly. They tucked up their dhoties, seized every available knife and crowbar, and began to hack the garden. Creepers, bushes, and lawns were laid low. What could not be trimmed was cut to the root. The inner walls of the house brightened with the unobstructed glare streaming in. When there was nothing more to be done Dasa asked triumphantly, 'Where is the snake?'

An old beggar cried for alms at the gate. They told her not to pester when they were engaged in a snake hunt. On hearing it the old woman became happy. 'You are fortunate. It is God Subramanya who has come to visit you. Don't kill the snake.' Mother was in hearty agreement: 'You are right. I forgot all about the promised Abhishekam. This is a reminder.' She gave a coin to the beggar, who promised to send down a snake-charmer as she went. Presently an old man appeared at the gate and announced himself as a snake-charmer. They gathered around him. He spoke to them of his life and activities and his power over snakes. They asked admiringly: 'How do you catch them?' 'Thus,' he said, pouncing upon a hypothetical snake on the ground. They pointed the direction in which the cobra had gone and asked him to go ahead. He looked helplessly about and said: 'If you show me the snake, I'll at once catch it. Otherwise what can I do? The moment you see it again, send for me. I live nearby.' He gave his name and address and departed.

Questions

5 Have we met any new characters?
6 What have we learned about the mother on this page?
7 And Dasa?
8 How do you think the story will develop?

70 At five in the afternoon, they threw away their sticks and implements and repaired to the veranda to rest. They had turned up every stone in the garden and cut down every grass blade and shrub, so that the tiniest insect coming into the garden should have no cover. They were loudly discussing the various measures they would take to protect themselves against reptiles in the future, when Dasa appeared before them carrying a water-pot whose mouth was sealed with a slab of stone. He put the pot down and said: 'I have caught him in
80 this. I saw him peeping out of it. I saw him before he could see me.'

He explained at length the strategy he had employed to catch and seal up the snake in the pot. They stood at a safe distance and gazed on the pot. Dasa had the glow of a champion on his face. 'Don't call me an idler hereafter,' he said. Mother complimented him on his sharpness and wished she had placed some milk in the pot as a sort of religious duty. Dasa picked up the pot cautiously and walked off
90 saying that he would leave the pot with its contents with the snake-charmer living nearby. He became the hero of the day. They watched him in great admiration and decided to reward him adequately.

It was five minutes since Dasa was gone when the youngest son cried: 'See there!' Out of a hole in the compound wall a cobra emerged. It glided along towards the gate, paused for a moment to look at the
100 gathering in the veranda with its hood half open. It crawled under the gate and disappeared along a drain. When they recovered from the shock they asked, 'Does it mean that there are two snakes here?' The college boy murmured: 'I wish I had taken the risk and knocked the water-pot from Dasa's hand; we might have known what it contained.'

R.K. Narayan: *A snake in the grass*

Thinking about the story

What was in the pot?

1 What did Dasa say was in the water pot?
2 Did the college boy believe him?
3 Do you think the others believed him?
4 What do you think was in the pot?

Sorting out what we know

5 This is a very short story, but we meet a large number of characters. Some of them are just mentioned, while others we get to know quite well, especially the mother, the 'college boy of the house' and Dasa. Make a table like this for each one, to sum up what we learn about them:

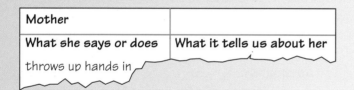

Mother	
What she says or does	What it tells us about her
throws up hands in	

How did they tell the story?

Each of the three characters you have been looking at had a different view of the story.

6 Look at the story from the viewpoint of the college boy.

  ■ Which parts of the story would he emphasise when he told other people about it?
  ■ Which parts would he pay less attention to?
  ■ What would he say about Dasa's part in the story?
  ■ How would he view the whole episode? (Would he be amused, angry, or what?)

7 Answer the same questions for the mother.
8 Now answer the same questions for Dasa.

A picture of a life

Like many of R.K. Narayan's stories, this story is set in a village deep in the Indian countryside. We learn a lot about the life of this family, but we also learn about the community of which it is a part.

Read it again and see how much you can find out about each of the topics listed below.

Write two or three sentences about each topic outlining what you have learned.

9 The physical surroundings: the house – the garden – the area beyond the garden.
10 The family: its daily life – relationships within it – the position of Dasa.
11 The local community: other people in the story – their positions in the local community.

The spider

Jan is known throughout the school as an expert teller of tall stories. Everyone loves Jan's stories but no one believes them. Then one day Jan finds an enormous spider down the back of a cupboard in the library. Strangely enough, it happens on the same day that there is a scare story on the radio about poisonous spiders turning up in imported crates of bananas. But Jan *really did* see a spider! Tell the story of what happens.

It sounds like 'a'

'Hate' and 'snake' half rhyme – they have the same vowel sound in the middle. See how good you are at spelling that sound. Copy the chart and fill in the blanks with words that spell the 'a' sound using those letters. See who is the first to fill all fifteen blanks!

a-e (as in *hate*)				
ay				
ai				
ey				
ei				
ea				

Wordsnake

All the blanks on this snake diagram make the names of snakes. You can find them somewhere in this unit. Copy the diagram and fill in the blanks.

B

O

A

C

O

G

TF

'I always wanted to be a writer'

Page	Title	What you do	Why you do it
22–23	**'I always wanted to be a writer'**	Discuss your favourite types of story and your least favourite, your favourite author, and the type of story you like to write.	To introduce the subject of the unit. To get you to think about reading and writing.
24–26	**A visit to Berlie's**	Read an interview with Berlie Doherty and answer questions about it. Try and find out as much as you can about buffer girls and other jobs that existed a long time ago.	To develop your skills as a reader. To learn about the life of a well-known author. To learn about the past.
27–28	**Past lives**	Look at photographs of child workers in the 19th century, choose one and talk about it. Make up the person's background. Write about a day in their life.	To use your imagination when thinking about the past. To practise planning a piece of writing. To develop your skills as a writer.
29–33	**Bridie and Jack**	Read a fiction extract from a story and answer questions about the characters.	To extend your ability to read fiction. To develop your vocabulary.
34–35	**Adjectives**	Learn to identify and use adjectives.	To increase your understanding of how sentences are constructed. To develop your vocabulary.
36–37	**Speech into writing**	Compare speech and writing. Practise turning a speech transcript into written English.	To understand the differences between speech and writing.
38–39	**Writing speech down**	Look at the extract and put the correct punctuation in.	To practise the punctuation of direct speech.
40	**Spelling: -able or -ible?**	Learn about the suffixes -able and -ible.	To improve your vocabulary and spelling.
40	**Wordpower**	Look again at some of the words in the unit.	To improve your vocabulary.

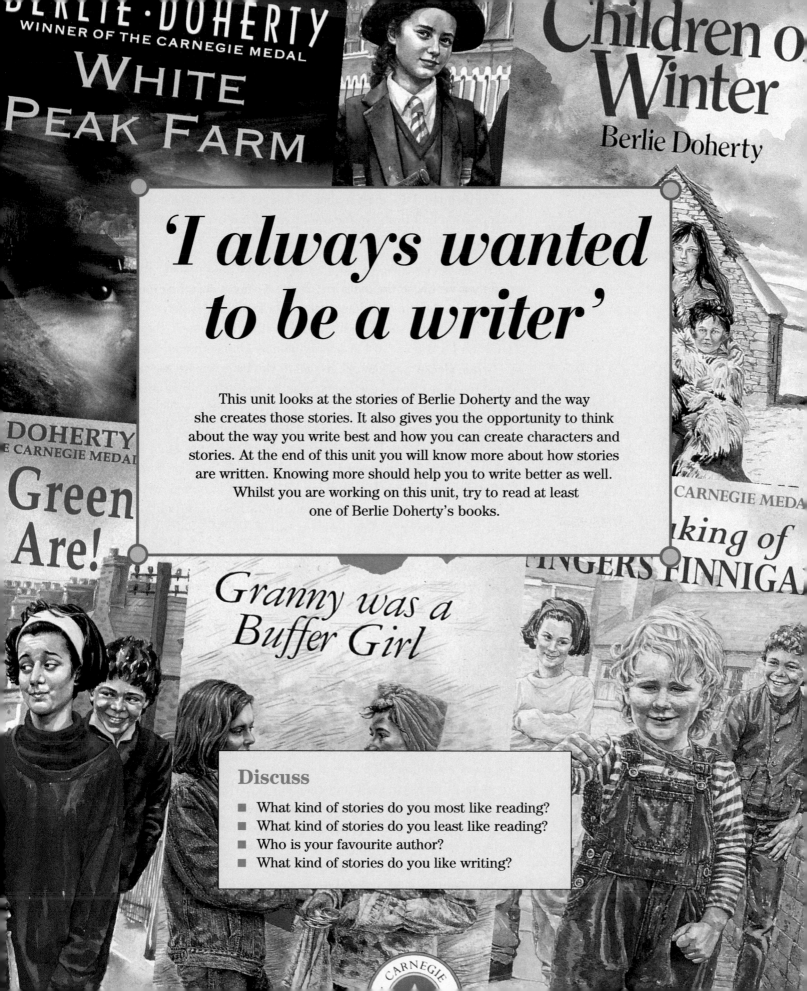

BERLIE·DOHERTY
WINNER OF THE CARNEGIE MEDAL
WHITE PEAK FARM

Children of Winter
Berlie Doherty

DOHERTY
E CARNEGIE MEDAL
Green Are!

CARNEGIE MEDA

Granny was a Buffer Girl

...king of
...NGERS FINNIGA

'I always wanted to be a writer'

This unit looks at the stories of Berlie Doherty and the way she creates those stories. It also gives you the opportunity to think about the way you write best and how you can create characters and stories. At the end of this unit you will know more about how stories are written. Knowing more should help you to write better as well. Whilst you are working on this unit, try to read at least one of Berlie Doherty's books.

Discuss

- What kind of stories do you most like reading?
- What kind of stories do you least like reading?
- Who is your favourite author?
- What kind of stories do you like writing?

CARNEGIE

A visit to Berlie's

Angela Harding,
Joanne Moorhouse
and Jennifer interview
Berlie Doherty.

It was a chilly, autumn afternoon when we went to talk to Berlie Doherty. As we travelled across Sheffield packed in our English teacher's Panda, at least one of us nursed the illusion that all writers live in mansions, so we were surprised to find Berlie in the front room of her comfortable semi-detached house in a Sheffield suburb.

We were welcomed by Berlie with chocolates (a recent birthday present!) and then we began the interview. Born in Knotty Ash, Liverpool, Berlie was the youngest of three children. Her older brother and sister (Denis and Jean) seemed like adults to her, rather than brother and sister: 'they were 16 and 13 when I was born, so I looked to them as being other adults'.

When Berlie was four she moved to Hoylake, 'where my first books were set. I lived in a house very much like the one on the front cover of *How green you are*. In fact it was that exact street. Five minutes' walk away was the sea. It was really nice. I was very lucky,' Berlie commented. 'I always wanted to be a writer most, but I can remember when I was little I had a list which I carried everywhere with me in my pocket. I wanted to be a writer, a singer, a ballet dancer (I never had dancing lessons, but I fancied myself as a dancer!), a swimming-pool attendant, an air hostess, or a librarian. I have done some singing, so I've achieved two of the things on my list. But I prefer writing.

'My serious writing started at a university course I went on to train to be a teacher. We were invited to write a story as part of the course. It was the first real thing I'd started. It was called *Requiem*. After finishing it recently, I didn't start writing again for ten months. I've actually been working at it for ten years, on and off.'

When she actually finishes a book she's sad. 'It's usually a matter of making myself stop writing, rather than making myself start. After I have finished I feel terrible. I feel grieved that I have lost someone close; a great deal of myself is in my books.

'I like to read all kinds of books. It's important to keep up with what's been written. I don't like to read escapist books though.'

Berlie's ideas come from just about everywhere. 'All kinds of things can give you an idea as a starting point. For instance, the idea for *Granny was a buffer girl* came from a painting in Graves Art Gallery, Sheffield. It was a painting of two buffer girls and it was the idea of these girls trapped forever in a painting, at the age of 18, which made me try to imagine what it would be like for them to step out of the painting and live real lives.'

'I always wanted to be a writer'

About her writing habits, she said, 'I start writing quite early after posting my letters, up until around lunchtime. I never write in the afternoon; I'd fall 40 asleep if I tried.

'I've got two favourite places. One is upstairs in my attic, which is where I usually work, and the other is Burbage Edge, where there is a big rock where I like to sit and write. If it's cold I just stay in the car and look down the valley. It doesn't always give me ideas, but it releases me. I just find it very relaxing to be there.

'When writing I always start off with a hand-written draft. I love that closeness to the page and the noise of the pen on the paper. I write on every other page and every other line. So I have lots of space for new ideas or to ask myself questions. Last of all I go to the word-processor and then it feels like a 50 proper, posh book. It's like a tapestry with all the threads woven in.'

Note
Berlie Doherty now lives in an isolated cottage in the country, and she writes in a barn overlooking the Pennines.
Requiem *started off as a short story but became the genesis of her first adult novel.*

Looking at the interview

1 What can you find out from the interview about Berlie Doherty's childhood?
2 What can you find out from the interview about the way that Berlie Doherty works as a writer?

Interviewing a writer

Imagine you had the chance to interview a well-known writer.

■ Who would you like to interview, and why?
■ What would you ask them? Decide on the ten questions you would most want to ask.

Study point

■ Berlie Doherty talks about the places where she works best. Find that part of the interview and read it again.
■ Make a list of good places for you to work and another list of those places that are not so good.

Research

Berlie talks in the interview about seeing an old painting of buffer girls in an art gallery and getting an idea for a book. What can you find out about buffer girls? What other jobs that existed 100 years ago do not exist today? See what you can discover.

Past lives

Look at the photographs on this page and then turn to page 28 to find out what to do.

Imagining a life

Pair work

- Choose one of the pictures to work on.
- Talk about what you can see in the photograph. What are your first impressions of:
  - the person or people
  - the place
  - the kind of work they do?

Individual work: the facts

TF

Work on the same picture, or choose another one.
   Make a list of all the facts you can work out about the person in the picture and the place where the picture was taken.

Work place
What it is like
The work s/he does

Imagining

Use your imagination about the person in the picture. Give the person a name, home and family.

Name
Age
Details of family background

Preparing to write

You are going to write about a day in the life of your character. Begin by working out what you think a typical day in his/her life would be like. Make a list of the main things that would happen.

What s/he thinks of the work
What s/he would like to do

Writing

Write a description of the day. Imagine that you are the character and write as if you were them.

Bridie and Jack

Berlie Doherty says that the story of Bridie Rooney and Jack Hall in *Granny was a buffer girl* is the story of her parents. Bridie's family are Catholics and believe it would be a sin for her to marry a Protestant. Jack's family are Protestants and disapprove of Catholics. Eventually they get married in secret during a lunch break from work. They have arranged to rent a flat but there are several days to wait until it is ready so they have to go home to their parents with the secret.

Jack was at home, brooding. He didn't know how to begin to tell his mother that he'd married a Catholic. Yet he couldn't bring himself to see Bridie again until he had told his mother, until he'd made it all right with her. Then he toyed with the idea of waiting till the time came for him to take his furnished room and just telling his mother he was moving in with a pal from work. Even that would hurt her. He sat by the fireside two nights after his wedding, prodding and prodding the coals to make them spurt, knowing nothing of what he was doing
10 but aware that his mother's sad eyes were fixed on him, and that he couldn't meet them.

'What's up with you, Jack?' she said to him at last.

'Nothing, Ma. L-leave me alone.' He cracked a coal open, so the flames burst through. Shadows flung frenzied arms across the walls and ceiling; his eyes were set deep into his face, in pockets of darkness. He'd never kept anything from her before. 'It would break her heart if I told her,' he thought to himself, while she watched him. 'But what am I doing, sitting here night after night, when I've a young wife waiting
20 for me?'

He flung the poker down and ran out. It rolled backwards and forwards on the hearth, backwards and forwards, till at last Jack's mother picked it up and stood it in its holder and went over to the window. She watched him, sorrowing for him, as he revved his motor-bike up in the yard.

'Where's the boy gone at this time of night?' her husband called, annoyed, from his study.

'He's not a boy,' she said. 'He's a grown man, Joseph. And he's sick with worry.'

Questions

1 Why is Jack upset?
2 Why doesn't he tell his mother?

30 Bridie was in bed when Jack arrived. He didn't know whether she slept in the front or the back of the house, so had no way of warning her. He banged on the door and Mr Rooney opened it to him.

'What's up?' he asked, not knowing Jack.

'I've c-come for B-B-Bridie.'

'What d'you mean, you've come for bloody Bridie?' The whole house was awake with the man's shouting.

Jack saw her on the stairs, and she gave him strength.

'She's my wife.'

40 He couldn't help smiling, in spite of his terror. Nor could she.

Mr Rooney turned round and pulled Bridie down to the door.

'Is this true?'

'Yes, Father,' she whispered. 'We were married Saturday.'

Mr Rooney stared at her, doubt and astonishment and rage chasing each other across his face. A surge of nostalgia swelled up in him. Nothing was dearer to him 50 than romance.

'How old are you, Bridie?' he asked his daughter.

'Twenty-one.'

'You're a child yet, for all that,' he said softly. 'You must take care of her, young man.'

He pushed Bridie out on to the doorstep and shut the door before the moisture in his eyes betrayed him.

'But, Father,' said Bridie, hammering on the door. 'I'm still in my nightie.'

60 'You've made your bed, my girl,' he said roughly, pushing to the bolts on the other side. 'Now you must lie on it.'

Questions

3 What were Mr Rooney's feelings when he heard that Bridie had married Jack secretly?

4 What do you think of the way he treated her?

'Now what do we do?' asked Bridie.

'We go and tell my parents,' said Jack. 'Together. We should have done it in the first place. We've done it all wrong.'

He took off his jacket and put it round her shoulders, and after a bit of revving and kicking and running up and down the street he got the Matchless started and they set off on the long ride to his parents' house. Bridie snuggled against his back and closed her eyes. He grinned.

70   'Happy?' he shouted.

She nodded and smiled cosily, even though she knew he couldn't see her doing it. He started singing, with the wind gasping into his breath and his voice jerking with every rut and stone on the road. 'I'd like to take you, on a slow boat to China.' And Bridie started laughing, shouting with laughing, and they knew that nothing as terrible and as wonderful as this would ever happen to them again.

Jack's mother heard them coming. 'Joseph,' she called. 'He's back.' She opened the door to them and she and her husband stood in the polished hallway in silence as Bridie and Jack came in, hand in hand, their singing

80 and their laughter quite gone.

'This is Bridie,' Jack said, looking at his father. 'She's a Catholic, and she's my wife.'

Bridie had oil on her nightie. Her hands and her cheeks were red with the wind and her hair was in a terrible state. Jack's father went back into the drawing-room, where they heard him putting his books back on their shelves.

'You can't stay here,' said Jack's mother to Bridie. 'I'm sorry.'

The three stood, saying nothing. Never before had Jack been so aware of the hall clock's loud tick.

90   'I've nothing else to wear,' said Bridie.

'Of course. Come up to my room and I'll find you something.'

Neither of the women looked at each other. Bridie followed Jack's mother up the polished stairs.

'We've nowhere to go,' said Jack when his mother came down again. 'We've a furnished room, but it's not ours till Saturday.' 'You have a good home here,' she reminded him. She joined her husband in the drawing-room.

More sad than angry, Jack went

100 upstairs and stuffed some clothes into his small knapsack. He'd no idea what they would do. He came out of his room again when he heard Bridie going downstairs. She was wearing one of his mother's best suits, a very

Questions

5 Why does Bridie think of what they are doing as 'terrible *and* wonderful'?

6 What do you think of the way Jack's parents react to the news?

expensive one in pale blue silk. He knew his mother would have asked her to wear it.

'You look lovely,' he said, helpless.

They stood in the doorway as Jack's parents came out of the drawing-room together. The old man's voice was steady and polite.

'There can be no question of your living here together,' he said. 'I regret your action, Jack. However, I acknowledge that you are now man and wife.' He was unable to continue, but handed Jack a wallet of money.

'Conscience money!' Bridie had her mother's temper. Jack put his hand on her arm. He knew what it had cost his parents to do this.

'You will find an hotel,' his mother said, 'and you will be able to have a honeymoon. We would both like that for you. And when you return, you will have your own home to go to, and that is best.'

They didn't see them out, though they listened to the sound of Jack's bike as it roared off down the drive away from their house and off along the road that led to Derbyshire, and for a long time after the sound of it had died away they still imagined they could hear it, and didn't speak.

Berlie Doherty: *Granny was a buffer girl*

Questions

7 What is your opinion now of how Jack's parents treated them?

8 How do you think his parents feel at the end of this extract?

Stories and feelings

There are six characters in this story: Bridie, Jack, and their parents. Bridie's parents are Mr and Mrs Rooney (although we don't meet Mrs Rooney here). Jack's parents are Mr and Mrs Hall. At each stage in the story we learn a lot about how the different characters feel about what is happening.

Finding the words

1 You are going to look more closely at how each of the main characters feels about the events of the story. Begin by making a chart like this:

Page	Bridie	Jack	Mr Rooney	Mrs Hall	Mr Hall

2 Now read page 29 again, thinking particularly about the feelings of Jack and his parents.
3 Use your table to list words that describe those feelings. (Don't forget that if you use words from the text, put them in quotation marks.) List as many words as you can.

Page	Bridie	Jack	Mr Rooney	Mrs Hall	Mr Hall
29		'brooding'		anxious	

4 Now do the same for the rest of the pages of the story.

Writing it up

You should now have a full set of notes about how each of the characters feels at each stage in the story.

5 Choose one of the characters.
6 Look carefully at your notes, and think about how that character has felt and behaved.
7 Write a few sentences describing the character's feelings and actions.
8 Now do the same for the other characters in the story.

A different point of view

9 We see the events of this story mainly from Jack's point of view. How do you think one of the parents might have told it? Imagine that Mr Hall, or Mrs Hall, or Mr Rooney meets a friend the next day and tells the whole story. Choose one of them and write his or her version of the story.

TF

Adjectives

Jack	Mr Rooney
worried	astonished

TF If you look at the list of words you made when you were working on page 33, you will probably find that they were adjectives.

People often say that adjectives are 'describing words'. Another way of checking whether a word is an adjective is to look at how it can be used. Most adjectives can be used in these ways:

■ they can come before a noun:
a ***strange*** story

■ they can come after words like *is* and *seem*:
*that story is **strange**.*

How strange?

Adjectives can often be changed in order to help make comparisons.

You might wish to compare two things, so you might say:
*Fact is often **stranger** than fiction.*

If you wanted to compare more than two things, you might tell someone:
*That is the **strangest** thing I have ever heard.*

So most adjectives have three forms:

adjective	comparative form	superlative form
strange	stranger	strangest
green	greener	greenest

Some adjectives cannot be changed so we use the words 'more' and 'most' in front of the adjective:

beautiful	more beautiful	most beautiful

Spotting adjectives

1 Look at the story on pages 29–32 and pick out five adjectives. Write them down.
2 Write down the comparative and superlative forms of three of them.

Note

You should only use the superlative when there are more than two.

You can say, for example:

Janet is the cleverest girl in our class. ✔

You should not say:

My sister Janet and I are both clever, but she is the cleverest. ✗

Using adjectives

When you worked on page 33, you probably quoted some adjectives from the story and added others you had thought of yourself. How many of the adjectives in this list did you use?

AGITATED
ALARMED ANXIOUS
RUFFLED
SHAKEN
BOTHERED HARASSED
TORMENTED
CONCERNED
CONFUSED TROUBLED
DISCONCERTED
DISTRESSED HAUNTED UNCOMFORTABLE
PERPLEXED
PERTURBED UNEASY
DISTURBED UNSETTLED
FLUSTERED RATTLED UPSET
WORRIED

Check the meanings

1 Look at the list and write down any of the words for which you do not know the meaning.
2 Use a dictionary to find out their meanings.

Suitable or not?

3 Which of the words in the list would be suitable to describe any of the characters in the story on pages 29–32?

Use them!

4 Choose two of the words in the list and for each one write a sentence that uses it correctly and shows its meaning clearly.

TF

Speech into writing

When you interview someone – as the three girls did on pages 24–25 – one of the difficult things is to remember everything you are told. You can make notes as the interview goes along – or write things down afterwards. Another way is to use a cassette recorder. If you do this, you have a record of *everything* the person says.

You might think that all you have to do then is write down their words. But it isn't as easy as that. We interviewed Berlie Doherty about her work. This is what she said about one of her books, *Tough luck*.

I went into this school...Hall Cross School...as writer in residence which involved – meant that I had to go in one day a week for a term and work with different classes so I was doing poetry and play-writing with different classes and I'd got this class of third years – or whatever they're called these days – Year 8... anyway...it's not third years any more I always used to be really scared of third years 'cos they giggle anyway as soon as I met them I liked them there was a lovely class feeling about them and I decided that I wasn't going to spend my eleven visits doing a series of eleven different writing exercises I'd like to do something sustained so just out of the top of my head I just said do you fancy writing a book and they said yes so I said OK you choose what the book's going to be about so they had a secret ballot and two-thirds of them voted for a book about themselves so there I was with this research material in front of me...absolutely marvellous...and we took – we spent the first session – I only spent eleven hours with them altogether – I spent – we spent the first session just talking really about being thirteen and

Reading aloud

It is quite difficult to make sense of what Berlie Doherty says if you try to read it silently. It is much better to read it aloud.

Work with a partner
1   Each of you choose a different section of about ten lines.
2   Read through your section and try to make sense of it.
3   Take it in turns to read your section aloud to your partner. Try to make it sound as much like real speech as you can.
4   Help each other by making comments and suggestions.
5   Practise until both sections are as good as you can make them.

Writing

Work on your own
1   Work on the same section of ten lines.
2   Study it carefully to see how it breaks down into sentences.
3   Write it out in correctly punctuated sentences. As you go, miss out any words that are repeated, or are not needed in writing.
4   You may find that you have to add one or two words so that the sentences are complete.

On the facing page you can see how the first few lines might be written down.

everything associated with it and their futures and their pasts, all kinds of things...um...then we decided that it would be about a class like theirs in a school like theirs but not their school and not them because they all wanted to be in it and I explained to them how difficult it is to write about people you actually know because you can't tell lies about them and writing fiction is all about telling lies and...um...that it's...it's easy to kind of start off kind of sideways on with somebody who is slightly familiar and then by the time you've turned them round as characters they've become someone in their own right so we just kind of invented a few characters who might represent the kind of person who might go to a school like that like the lad who doesn't turn up to lessons, the twagger.

Spoken

I went into this school...Hall Cross School...as writer in residence which involved – meant that I had to go in one day a week for a term and work with different classes so I was doing poetry and play-writing with different classes

Written

I went into Hall Cross School as writer in residence which meant that I had to go in one day a week for a term and work with different classes. So I was doing poetry and play-writing with different classes.

So what's the difference?

Compare your written version with the spoken words.

1 What are the main differences between the two?
2 Why do you think there are these differences – what causes them?

Writing speech down

Speech can be written down in a number of ways. In a play it is written as script. It is unusual to use script in a prose story, but some writers have done it, and it can be effective. In a story, conversation is usually presented as direct speech, or as reported speech.

Punctuating direct speech

Every **new** piece of speech starts with a capital letter, even if it is not the first word in the sentence.

When there is a new speaker, start a new line and indent.

If a piece of speech comes in the middle of a sentence it must have a comma, or a colon before the opening inverted comma(s).

> She hurried away from her tram-stop, rounded her street, saw a triangle of light thrown across the cobbles, and knew he was on the doorstep.
>
> 'What time d'you call this, you little hussy?' His voice echoed round the houses.
>
> 'Half past nine, Dad.' She knew it was no use lying. Lying was just as much a sin as disobedience was.
>
> 'Get in that house and up them stairs to your bed!'
>
> She dodged under his arm and ran across the room where her brother Will was preparing his bath in front of the fire, and her mother sat darning at the table.
>
> 'Up them stairs!' roared her father as Bridie stopped

Each piece of speech begins and ends with inverted commas: single : ' ' or double: " "

Every piece of speech ends with a punctuation mark **before** the closing inverted comma(s). If it is the end of a sentence, use a full stop, question mark, or exclamation mark. If the sentence is going on, use a comma, a question mark or an exclamation mark.

You try

This extract tells only part of the story in the pictures. Tell the rest of it, using correctly punctuated direct speech.

Spelling: -able or -ible?

These two suffixes can cause people problems with spelling. The problem is that there is no clear rule. But the following advice may help:

-able

All new words that are formed are spelled **-able.**

skateboard → skateboardable

If the letter before the suffix is a hard 'c' or 'g', then the suffix is **-able.**

practicable

Usually if you can remove the suffix and are still left with a proper word, then the suffix should be **-able.**

affordable → afford

-ible

If you take the suffix away and what is left is not a proper word, then the suffix should usually be **-ible.**

possible → poss

The list of words ending in **-ible** is quite short and some of them are not very well known.

These are the commonest words ending in **-ible:**

accessible	admissible	audible
collapsible	credible	edible
flexible	horrible	incredible
invisible	legible	possible

Wordpower

All these words are in the unit you have been reading.

1 Explain the meanings of as many as you can.
2 For those you cannot explain, find them in the unit and try to work out their meaning from the sentence they are in. Then check them in a dictionary.
3 If there are any left, look them up in the dictionary.
4 Make sure that you can spell them.

word	page	line	word	page	line	word	page	line
illusion	24	3	librarian	24	18	Requiem	24	23
tapestry	25	50	escapist	24	31	word-processor	25	49
moisture	30	56	frenzied	29	14	brooding	29	1
betrayed	30	57	sorrowing	29	24	hearth	29	22
snuggled	31	69	conscience	32	115	nostalgia	30	49

LOST IN TIME

It all started when Mum asked me to clear out an old cupboard. We'd only just moved into this old house and the last people had left all sorts of rubbish behind.

The cupboard was in a spare room that we'd just filled up with all the packing cases and stuff we couldn't find anywhere to put when we moved in. Junk, in fact. But there were two big cupboards and Mum thought if I emptied them we could put some of the stuff in there.

I didn't really want to do it, but she said she'd give me some extra pocket

DON'T TURN OVER!
What do you think happens next? Make up the next part of the story.

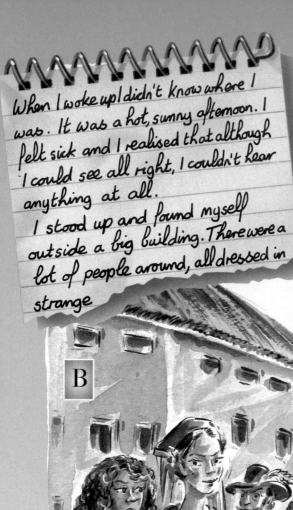

When I woke up I didn't know where I was. It was a hot, sunny afternoon. I felt sick and I realised that although I could see all right, I couldn't hear anything at all.

I stood up and found myself outside a big building. There were a lot of people around, all dressed in strange

WHAT'S GOING ON?

Looking for clues

Work in a group

1 Look carefully at the pictures above and on page 42. What clues can you find to tell you *when* the people in them lived?

- Look at the clothes they are wearing.
- Look at the building in picture **B** – what is it?
- What is going on in picture **E**?

2 Look again for clues that tell you *where* they are.

Thinking about the clues

3 Now work out where the girl is and roughly what the date is. You may need to do some research:

- What kinds of book do you need to look in?
- Where will you find them?
- Are there any other sources of information you could use?

Thinking about the story

4 Think about the following:

- How did she get there?
- What is the link between these pictures and what happened on page 41?
- What do you think the people speaking are saying?

Tell her story

Work on your own
Use the ideas you have built up so far to continue the girl's story. Write as if you were her ('I...').

They dragged me away. I tried to scream, but the bag they had put over my head muffled the sound and one of them hit me. Then I was thrown to the ground. It was inside a building, I think, I couldn't see anything. There were people talking

1 What's that to thee? Now knaves. Bind fast her hands and legs.

2 Aye sir.

3 Why – sell her thou foolish knave. Sell her to some great man of substance as a servant or a slave.

4 Have ye the child?

5 In London, my lord?

6 Let's see, let's see. A pretty child. And one that will attract the highest price.

7 And stop her mouth. Here: use this kerchief.

8 Why, no, my lord. Your lordship expressly did forbid it.

9 Aye, my lord.

12 What would my lord with this little child?

10 Now guard her safe till my return.

11 I trust she is still well? You have not harmed her in the course of taking her?

CONFUSION!

As you can see, the girl is so confused that the conversation is all jumbled up.

Work in a group
1 Decide how many people you think are actually speaking. Is it two, three, or four?
2 Work out the order in which the speeches come. Write the numbers down in that order.
3 Now try acting the conversation. Use the speeches that are printed, but if you wish, add extra speeches.

What language?

Look carefully at the language used in the speeches and think about the ways in which it differs from the way you speak.

1 Are there any words you found unusual? If so, write them down, and for each one, think of a more common word that means much the same thing.
2 Are any of the sentences constructed in a strange way? If so, how would *you* express the same idea in a sentence?

Writing

Work on your own
1 Write a script based on the work you did in your group.
2 Now tell this part of the girl's story, writing as 'I...'

I can't remember much about the next few hours, I think I must have dozed off. I woke up when I felt myself being lifted and then they half-dragged and half-carried me out of the building. (I know that, because there was fresh air and I could hear street sounds.)
They must have taken me quite a long way. Then suddenly they threw me down onto a hard surface. I didn't know where I was, but it seemed strange. I could feel a sort of rocking movement and heard a strange noise that sounded like water slopping around. Apart from the

What happens next?

1 Look for the clues in this part of the girl's story.
2 Make a list of them.
3 What does each one tell you?
4 Decide:

   ■ where they have taken her
   ■ why
   ■ what might happen next.

5 Now tell the next part of her story.

My hands and feet were tied and I still could not see. I struggled and struggled to get free and at last the ropes on my wrists began to work a bit loose. In the end I managed to get my hands free and then untie my feet, pull off the old bag and the gag

ESCAPE?

These pictures suggest a number of different ways in which the story might continue. As you can see, whichever one you choose, in the end the girl remembers the ring and decides to see if its magic powers will work again.

1 Decide which of the three routes you wish to follow. If you choose **A** or **C**, make up a story that uses the picture you are given. Using Route **B**, you can invent your own story.
2 Whichever route you choose, your story should end with the girl deciding to use the ring again.
3 Tell the story as if you were the girl.

WHAT NEXT?

These pictures suggest three different ways in which the story might continue after the girl has used the ring.

1 Look at each one carefully and think about how the story shown in that picture could develop.
2 Choose the picture you think offers the best story.
3 Tell that story as if you were the girl.

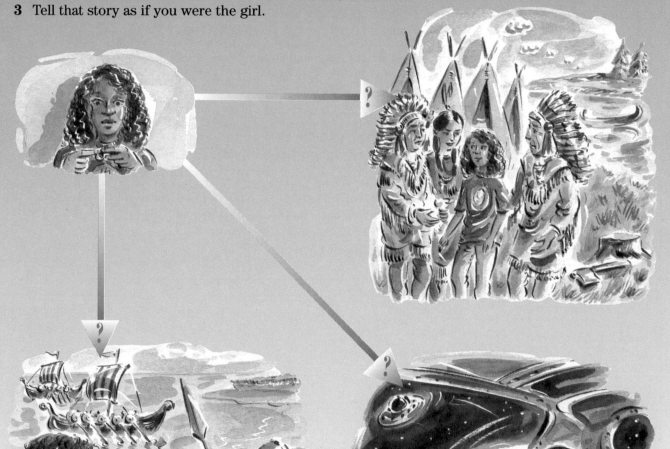

Boys and girls come out to play

Page	Title	What you do	Why you do it
49	**Boys and girls come out to play**	Think about the traditional male and female roles. Look at the comments and think about them.	To introduce the theme of the unit.
50–54	**A guide to a happy family Christmas**	Read the story then look at the pictures and think about how it is written and why.	To develop your skills as a reader and a writer. To learn about irony and satire.
55	**What's missing?**	Look at the sentences given and fill in the missing words. Think about how and why words and sentences are shortened.	To learn about making notes.
56–57	**Verbs: the whole story?**	Find verbs and verb phrases. Identify different parts of a verb phrase.	To learn about verbs and verb phrases. To understand more fully how sentences work.
58–59	**The lost son**	Read a story from the bible and a poem based on it. Compare the two and think about both of them. Re-tell the story from a different point of view.	To develop your skills as a reader and writer.
60–61	**Listn Big Brodda Dread, Na!**	Read a poem out loud and discuss the way it sounds.	To develop your reading and writing skills. To learn about different dialects.
62–63	**Indignation and tears down among the ferrets**	Read the story and answer the questions.	To improve your ability to read in detail.
64	**Punctuation revision**	Look back at what you have learnt on punctuation and capital letters.	To improve your punctuation.
65	**Spelling revision**	Look back at what you have learnt about spelling and plurals.	To improve your spelling.

Boys and girls
come out to play

'My dad doesn't even mow the lawn. The only work he does is to turn the television on and off.'

'The stronger people are, the more work they ought to do. As most men are stronger than most women, they ought to do more work, especially at home.'

'Everyone should have a chance, but I don't see why boys should be forced to learn dancing or sewing or cooking. It's supposed to be a free country.'

'My mum went to night classes and now she mends the car...which is more than Dad ever did.'

'Boys shouldn't have to do the washing up. That's women's work.'

Responding

- What sort of work have boys and men traditionally done?
- What sort of work have girls and women traditionally done?
- What do you think of the comments on this page about men and women?
- What do you think about giving people equal opportunities?

A guide to a happy family Christmas

7am

Daughter woken up to help her mother stuff the turkey and put it in the oven. Given the unpleasant task of taking the giblets out of the not-quite-defrosted turkey without using rubber gloves. Father and son sleeping upstairs.

8am

Daughter goes upstairs to have a bath to get rid of the sage and onion stuffing smell. Her brother is having his morning shower and has used up the hot water. He has also used her towel which he has left in a soggy heap on the bathroom floor.

8.30am

10 Stocking time. Daughter's stocking contains knickers, a copy of *Just Seventeen*, a bar of soap, a pack of Bic razors for her legs and a tube of toothpaste. Son's stocking contains a new car for his Scalextric set, a special memorial England World Cup Subbuteo team with an authentic crying Gazza, a blank video cassette to record those Christmas re-runs and his first Philips electric razor. It has a special LCD showing him how many shaving hours he has left.

9am

Father and son go and try out new razor. Mother and daughter go to check on the turkey and to set the table.

10am

20 Father decides it is time to get the drinks tray ready for the guests who will be arriving in less than three hours. Generally gets in the way in the kitchen, puffing and panting as he puts some glasses on a tray. Complains about having to do so much work. Son given the all-important job of filling the ice bucket with ice.

11am

Father and son are relaxing in front of the television, exhausted after sorting out the drinks. Father decides it is time to light the fire. He goes through to find it has already been lit. Says it will

30 never keep going. It does.

11.30am

Red alert. One of the lights on the Christmas tree has blown. Son turns off the lights at the wall while father tries to find out which bulb has gone.

Boys and girls come out to play

12.30pm

Defective bulb located. New bulb put in. Son turns on plug and all the lights in the house go out. Mother locates fuse box and manages to mend fuse. Father says it will never keep going. It does.

12.45pm

Three aunts, two uncles, one grandmother arrive. Son sets video to record the World Cup special. Mother, daughter, aunts and grandmother retire to kitchen to look at the turkey. Son puts ice in his uncle's whisky.

1 pm

Lunch is ready. Father, son and uncles retrieved from playing Subbuteo. Father looks for carving knife. It is next to the turkey. Father complains that he wasn't told that.

1.05pm

Father starts carving turkey. This is the first time that he has actually set eyes on it but that doesn't stop him saying it took him no effort to cook it. This is true. His wife and daughter did it.

1.10pm

Son given the all-important task of pouring the wine. His aunts comment on how much he has grown and how much use he is around the house. He smiles. Daughter is still in the kitchen having burnt her hand taking the potatoes out of the oven. She enters and nobody notices.

1.50pm

Son pours brandy on Christmas pudding which his sister has just taken out of the oven. Lights it, burning his sister's hand again. Carries it through to his family who applaud loudly. Sister enters with plates and no one notices.

2.30pm

Son tells family about what his hopes for the future are. Daughter puts the coffee on. Son fetches his new razor to show his uncle. Passed around the table whilst daughter passes coffee cups round.

3pm

Daughter doing the washing-up. Mother showing aunts around the garden. Son racing his uncle at Scalextric. His uncle crashes five times.

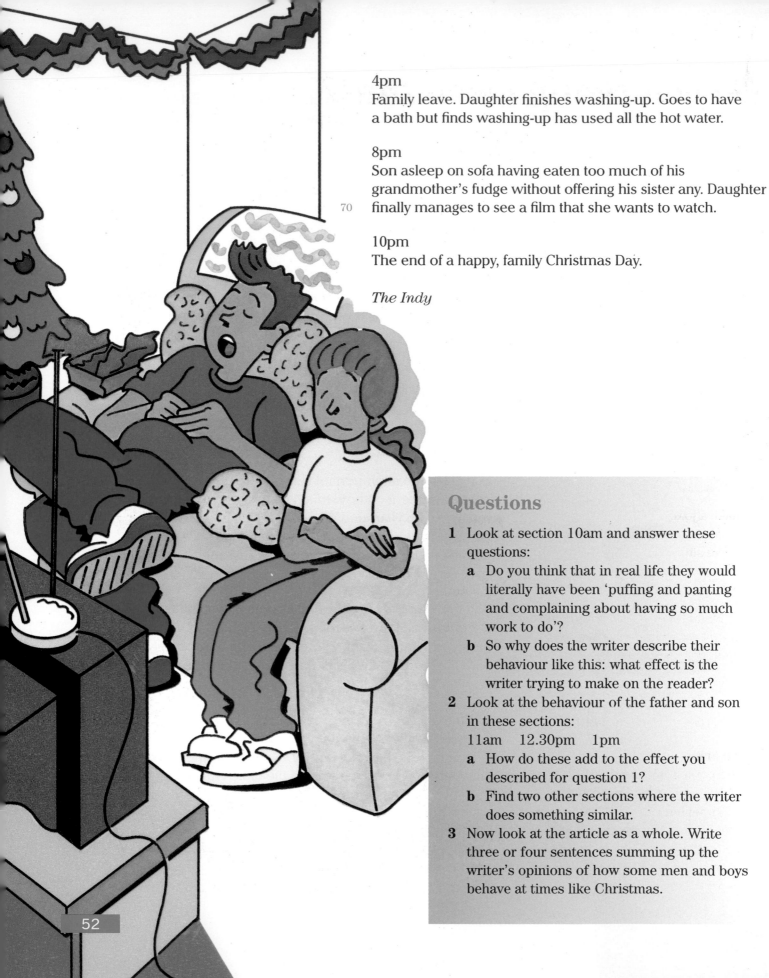

4pm

Family leave. Daughter finishes washing-up. Goes to have a bath but finds washing-up has used all the hot water.

8pm

70 Son asleep on sofa having eaten too much of his grandmother's fudge without offering his sister any. Daughter finally manages to see a film that she wants to watch.

10pm

The end of a happy, family Christmas Day.

The Indy

Questions

1 Look at section 10am and answer these questions:
   a Do you think that in real life they would literally have been 'puffing and panting and complaining about having so much work to do'?
   b So why does the writer describe their behaviour like this: what effect is the writer trying to make on the reader?

2 Look at the behaviour of the father and son in these sections:
   11am   12.30pm   1pm
   a How do these add to the effect you described for question 1?
   b Find two other sections where the writer does something similar.

3 Now look at the article as a whole. Write three or four sentences summing up the writer's opinions of how some men and boys behave at times like Christmas.

Do you really mean that?

'Son given **all-important** job of filling the ice-bucket with ice'

Using irony

Sometimes we say one thing and mean another. In the picture on the right, for example, the girl doesn't really mean 'Thank you very much'. She wants to tell her 'friend' just how annoyed she is about what she has done to her tennis racket. She does this by saying the *opposite* of what she means, and using a particular tone of voice.

People often say one thing and mean something very different. They may do it to:

- make a joke
- make someone or something sound silly
- hurt another person's feelings
- make someone feel small

or for many other reasons. It's a way of playing with words. It is called 'using irony', or 'being ironic'.

What did they say and how did they say it?

Pair work
1 Choose one of the pictures.
2 With your partner, discuss what is happening.
3 Decide what the speaker might say if s/he wanted to be ironic.
4 Practise saying it so that you get the right tone of voice.

Now do the same thing for the other pictures.

Back to that family Christmas

Satire

The article you have been reading is an example of satire: *sending up* someone or something that you want to make fun of.

1 Think of some kind of behaviour that you think should be satirised – something that you would like to send up. Be clear in your mind exactly what it is that you dislike about that behaviour.

2 Imagine what it would be like if people went much much further with this kind of behaviour – what kind of crazy situations might develop?

3 Choose an exaggerated situation like this and describe it solemnly and seriously, as if it was really happening.

satire *noun*
(a) the use of mocking or exaggerated humour to ridicule faults and vices
(b) a piece of writing, song, etc. which does this
satirical (**say** sa-**tirri**-k'l) or **satiric** (*adjective*)
(a) of, like or containing satire: 'a *satirical* book' **(b)** using or fond of satire: 'a *satirical* author'

What's missing?

Part of the attraction of the article on pages 50–52
is the way in which it is written. Look at these sentences:

- Father and son go and try out new razor.
- Father and son sleeping upstairs.
- Father starts carving turkey.
- Mother showing aunts around the garden.

Each sentence has one or more words missing from it.

1 Work out what the missing words are.
2 Write the sentences out in full, adding the missing words.
3 Why do you think the article was written in the way it was?

In brief

½ lb sausages
tin toms
Trolls

England thrashed
Port-of-Spain, Trinidad
Any hope of an England victory disappeared

Y REG
FORD SIERRA 1600
4 dr HATCH
BEIGE...£595

Each of these snippets uses shortened forms of language.
For each one explain:

- how it is shortened
- why it has been done.

Can you think of other examples?

Making notes

When you are studying subjects at school, you sometimes have
to write 'in brief'. Different teachers may ask you to do this in
different ways. Look at the writing you have done recently for
different subjects and make a table like this:

| TF |

Subject	Writing in brief?	What it is called	How we do it
History	✓	Making notes	We read the textbook and then write down a short version of what it says – in proper sentences.

Verbs: the whole story?

1 Copy out this short extract from the article and underline the verbs.

For example: Daughter <u>woken</u> up to …

> **7am**
> Daughter woken up to help her mother stuff the turkey and put it in the oven. Given the unpleasant task of taking the giblets out of the not-quite-defrosted turkey without using rubber gloves. Father and son sleeping upstairs.

2 Now write the sentences out again, in full – adding all the words necessary to make them into full sentences.

3 Underline the verbs in your revised version.

For example: Daughter <u>is woken</u> up to …

4 Compare the two sets of verbs: what changes have taken place?

The verb phrase

The verb in a sentence may be just one word, or it may be a group of words. The verbs in these sentences have been printed in bold:

*Anna **finished** a story last week.*
*She **is starting** another one now.*
*She **has been writing** stories since she was seven.*

> The word **verb** is used in two different ways:
>
> - it is a word class, and is used to describe single words just as **adjective**, and **noun** are
> - it is part of a sentence.
>
> To help avoid confusion, when we mean the verb in a sentence, we call it the **verb phrase**.

List them

Make a list of the verb phrases from this text:

> One of the most exciting things you can see is an electrical storm at night, when the sky is lit up by repeated flashes of lightning, and your ears are deafened by thunder. Lightning flashes can be enormous. In flat country they are often 6 kilometres in length and they may be as much as 30 kilometres.

> People say that lightning never strikes twice in the same place, but this is not true. It can strike more than once and in fact there are people who have been struck by lightning a number of times. The world record holder is an American, Roy C. Sullivan. His experiences of lightning began in 1942. During his lifetime he was struck a total of seven times.

Parts of the verb phrase EXT

Look at your list of verb phrases. Some of them contain one word and some of them contain more than one:

one word	more than one
began	can see

A verb phrase always contains a **full** verb, like *see*. Nearly all full verbs have meanings that you can explain to somebody. For example, if a foreigner asked you the meaning of *see*, you could explain, or show them what it means. So *see* is a full verb.

The verb phrase may also contain one or more **auxiliary** verbs. These do not have a meaning that you can explain or show, but they help the full verb to express its meaning.

auxiliary verbs	full verbs
may	chase
will	munch

Warning

There are two verbs that can be full verbs **or** auxiliary verbs:

is/am etc
have/had etc

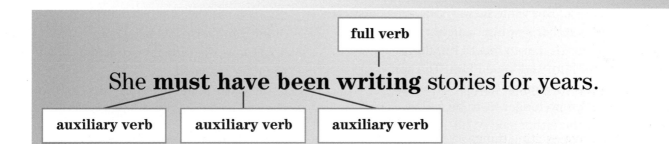

Separate them

Look at the list of verb phrases you wrote for page 56. Separate them into full and auxiliary verbs like this:

auxiliary	full
can	see

The lost son

There was once a man who had two sons; and the younger said to his father, 'Father, give me my share of the property.' So he divided his estate between them. A few days later the younger son turned the whole of his share into cash and left home for a distant country, where he squandered it in reckless living. He had spent it all when a severe famine fell upon that country and he began to feel the pinch. So he went and attached himself to one of the local landowners, who sent him onto his farm to mind the pigs. He would have been glad to fill his belly with the pods that the pigs were eating; and no one gave him anything. Then he came to his senses and said, 'How many of my father's paid servants have more food than they can eat, and here am I, starving to death! I will set off and go to my father, and say to him, "Father, I have sinned, against God and against you; I am no longer fit to be called your son; treat me as one of your paid servants."' So he set out for his father's house. But while he was still a long way off his father saw him, and his heart went out to him. He ran to meet him, flung his arms round him, and kissed him. The son said, 'Father, I have sinned, against God and against you; I am no longer fit to be called your son.' But the father said to his servants, 'Quick! fetch a robe, my best one, and put it on him; put a ring on his finger and shoes on his feet. Bring the fatted calf and kill it, and let us have a feast to celebrate the day. For this son of mine was dead and has come back to life; he was lost and is found.' And the festivities began.

Now the elder son was out on the farm; and on his way back, as he approached the house, he heard music and dancing. He called one of the servants and asked what it meant. The servant told him, 'Your brother has come home, and your father has killed the fatted calf because he has him back safe and sound.' But the elder son was angry and refused to go in. His father came out and pleaded with him; but he retorted, 'You know how I have slaved for you all these years; I never once disobeyed your orders; and you never gave me so much as a kid, for a feast with my friends. But now that this son of yours turns up, after running through your money with his women, you kill the fatted calf for him.' 'My boy,' said the father, 'you are always with me, and everything I have is yours. How could we help celebrating this happy day? Your brother here was dead and has come back to life, was lost and is found.'

Elizabeth Seely: *retold from the New Testament*

What do you think:

- of the younger son's behaviour
- about how the father treated him when he returned
- of the older son's reaction
- the rest of the family thought of it all
- happened next?

Boys and girls come out to play

The prodigal son

1: Prodigal son
Better put on a bit of a show;
The old man will like that.
The real hurt is buried inside:
After the feast, tomorrow,
Back in the fields, grubbing about,
Knowing now there's no escape.

2: Brother
Better put on a bit of a sulk
10 Though really I'm glad he's back.
No one talked about him. We
Stepped over the gaps, closed
The spaces he had left. It was dull:
Just work, and silence.

3: Mother
These men, acting their parts:
Gestures larger than life – repentance,
Forgiveness, jealousy – to draw all
The attention away from their pain.
20 My daughters make no fuss, and I,
I have disappeared from the story.

Michael Harrison

Digging below the surface

TF

Michael Harrison has dug below the surface of the story of the younger son by looking at the whole family. Read the poem again and imagine what the family's life was like:

- before the younger son left
- while he was away
- after his return.

Telling the story

Now tell the story of what happened 'After the celebration' as if you were one of the following:

- the mother
- one of the daughters
- a neighbour and friend of the family.

These men...

1 What is the mother saying about the differences between men and women?
2 Do you agree with her?
3 Can you think of other stories – fact or fiction – that would back up what she is saying?
4 Can you think of stories that would contradict what she is saying?

Listn big brodda dread, na!

My sista is younga than me.
My sista outsmart five-foot three.
My sista is own car repairer
and yu nah catch me doin judo with her.

I sey I wohn get a complex.
I wohn get a complex.
Then I see the muscles my sista flex.

My sista is tops at disco dance.
My sista is well into self-reliance.
10   My sista plays guitar and drums
and wahn see her knock back double rums.

I sey I wohn get a complex.
I wohn get a complex.
Then I see the muscles my sista flex.

My sista doesn mind smears of grease and dirt.
My sista'll reduce yu with sheer muscle hurt.
My sista says no guy goin keep her phone-bound –
with own car mi sista is a wheel-hound.

I sey I wohn get a complex.
20   I wohn get a complex.
Then I see the muscles my sista flex.

James Berry

Reading aloud

Work on a group reading of the poem.

1 Discuss the **pattern** of the poem and what you want it to sound like.
2 Discuss how to divide it into sections for reading – and how each section should be read. (One voice? More than one voice? Quiet? Loud?)
3 Decide who will read each section.
4 Try it out.
5 Discuss how the reading went and what you need to do to improve it.
6 Continue in this way until you are satisfied with your performance.

What is the message?

1 Who is speaking in the poem?
2 What is the 'complex' that the speaker 'wohn get'?
3 What 'muscles' does the 'sista' flex?
4 Look at all the things the 'sista' can do. Why do they dismay the speaker?
5 Do you think that they are all things that girls should *want* to be good at?
6 What message is the poet wanting to put across?

The sound of the poem

The poet has written the poem in a way that helps you 'hear' how it should sound. You can see this if you compare these two versions of the first line. Try reading each of them aloud:

My sista is younga than me.
My sister is younger than me.

1 Find all the other words that have been spelled in an unusual way. Try saying each one twice:

■ as it might be spoken by a television newsreader
■ as it has been written.

The language of the poem

The poem is in dialect. It contains expressions that do not exist in Standard English. For example:

My sista is own car repairer

In Standard English this would be:

My sister repairs her own car

2 Find other examples of dialect expressions. For each one explain what it would be in Standard English.

Indignation and tears down among the ferrets

ON A COLD, crisp winter's morning, Sadie Roberts, 19, takes her three ferrets, Fitch, Flash and Ferris, and heads for the teeming burrows of Warren Hill near her village home in west Dorset.

Since the hunting season opened on 1 October, she has caught hundreds of rabbits. 'Farmer Buckler's got sheep there so he's glad someone keeps down the rabbit population,' she said. 'And Wells, the butcher in Bridport, buys them eight at a time at £1.50 each.'

Apart from bell-ringing and occasional work as a milk maid, Ms Roberts devotes her waking hours to her ferrets

10 which live, incongruously, among cages of pet rabbits in the garden of her council house.

Ms Roberts is one of many female ferret keepers and is angry over a feud sparked by sexism. She is a member of the National Ferret Welfare Society, known as 'the National', set up nearly a decade ago to counteract the ferret's image as a killer that does awful things up trouser legs. It has 1,200 members and most of its officers are women.

The feud came to a head at last year's annual meeting.

20 Kim Lathaen, the National's president and secretary, and newsletter editor, said she was fed up with being called 'that bloody woman', offered her resignation and burst into tears. Stunned officials persuaded her to stay but women ferreters around the country are still indignant about her treatment.

Ms Roberts, for one, fired off a letter of support to the newsletter. 'I am only a young lady at 19 years old and living in a little pocket of rabbit-ridden Dorset,' she wrote. 'I've been looked upon as a saviour these last two years by farmers and landowners alike for mounting my own "rabbit

30 control". Not once have I been frowned on by the aforesaid for being female.'

'Hedgerow moochers, I call them,' she said of Mrs Lathaen's critics last week. 'I met one at a game fair this year, an absolute know-all. He'd say things like, "Don't eat Indian curry and handle ferrets because they'll bite you on the nose".'

Mary Neale, the National's membership secretary, who runs a ferret sanctuary in Bedford, is equally dismissive of hedgerow moochers. 'A lot

of them put about this nonsense that ferrets don't
work so well if they're castrated and this is
definitely another attitude of male chauvinist
piggery,' she says.

'One man very sanctimoniously said to me, "I
think everything was put on this earth to multiply"
and I just glared at him and said, "Oh, come on,
this is 1993." They're the kind of man in sleeveless
vests, with horrible beer bellies and a can of ale in
one hand. They hang around show tents saying,
"Do you work your ferrets, mate?" '

Mrs Lathaen, from Henley-on-Thames, says she
has suffered years of prejudice inside and outside
the National, even though she has wide experience
as a ferreter, handles birds of prey and is often
called upon to give expert evidence in court cases
involving dangerous dogs. Her latest coup has
been an invitation to act as adviser to a new ferret
club set up at Eton College, with access to Lord
Napier's estate, Windsor Great Park. Old ferreters
have found her to be disconcertingly steely. She
makes them look foolish by publishing their
spluttering letters with the spelling mistakes and
wayward punctuation.

She is pessimistic about a change in attitudes. 'I changed my mind
about resigning because it's my baby and I couldn't bear to lose it,' she
said. 'We aren't going to change those dyed-in-the-wool ferreters who've
had it handed down for generations that ferrets should be kept in the
world of men.'

The Independent

Reading and understanding

1 Who is Sadie Roberts?
2 What does she spend most of her time doing?
3 Why is she angry?
4 Who is Kim Lathaen?
5 What happened to her that made women
  ferreters angry?
6 How does she make old ferreters look silly?
7 What does the writer mean by saying that
  Sadie Roberts' ferrets 'live, incongruously,
  among cages of pet rabbits'?

8 Why was 'the National' set up?
9 What was the point of Sadie's letter?
10 What are 'hedgerow moochers' and why
  do these women not like them?
11 Two explanations are given of why Kim Lathaen
  withdrew her resignation. What are they?
12 Read through the article again and make a list
  of the criticisms that women ferreters make
  against those who believe that ferrets 'should
  be kept in the world of men'.

Punctuation revision

Full stops and capital letters

1   In this passage, all the full stops and capital letters have been missed out. Write out the passage, putting in all the necessary full stops and capital letters.

> when mrs hopkins left to have a baby, 1 set 2 had a new teacher for english the new teacher was soft and did a lot of grinning you could tell her *anything* they called her smiler she smiled on and on, even when they made a racket 1 set 2 thought she wasn't quite right in the head
>
> on this particular morning, the boys came charging into smiler's room before the girls, hot-foot from registration some pulled up abruptly as they crashed across the threshold, as if an imaginary rider had yanked hard on an imaginary rein

Direct speech

2   The next section contains direct speech. Write out this section, adding all the necessary punctuation.

> they looked across at smiler but she never said go out and form a line and do it *properly* this time she just smiled on
>
> miss, miss! yelled gary radford, flapping the air with adventures in science, issue 1 he was building it up into an encyclopaedia will you read us a bit out of this it's dead good – all about shc
>
> shc? smiled smiler, raising an eyebrow and scratching her nose what's shc?
>
> spontaneous human combustion it says this man went up in flames when he was just sitting on the *bog* it says it's caused by stress

Rules

3   Now, in your own words, explain the rules governing when to use:

   ■ full stops
   ■ capital letters.

Spelling revision

Plurals in -s

1 Write out the plural of each of these words.

hero	bush	radiator	day	sky
gas	motto	box	zoo	desk
quiz	match	Eskimo	toy	
tomato	kangaroo	baby	volcano	

2 Explain the rules for adding endings to make the plural of words:

- that end in -y
- that end in -o
- that end in -s

-ible or -able?

3 Make each of these into a word by adding **-ible** or **-able**:

poss-	work-	flex-	sens-
afford-	horr-	cap-	practic-

Wordpower

All these words are in the unit you have been reading.

1 Explain the meanings of as many as you can.
2 For those you cannot explain, find them in the unit and try to work out their meaning from the sentence they are in. Then check them in a dictionary.
3 If there are any left, look them up in the dictionary.
4 Make sure you can spell them.

word	page	line	word	page	line	word	page	line
giblets	50	3	estate	58	4	authentic	50	13
locate(d)	51	36	squander(ed)	58	7	aforesaid	62	30
retrieve(d)	51	44	feud	62	13	dismissive	62	37
famine	58	8	decade	62	15	sanctimoniously	63	42
robe	58	30	counteract	62	15	coup	63	54
retort(ed)	58	46	saviour	62	28	steely	63	58
gesture(s)	59	17	castrate(d)	63	39	pessimistic	63	62

Treasure Island

Page	Title	What you do	Why you do it
67	**Treasure Island**	Read about Robert Louis Stevenson and see if you can do a short quiz about his life.	To start you thinking about the themes of the unit.
68	**Strange arrival**	See how much you can discover about a character from a short extract.	To improve your skills as a reader.
69–72	**The key to the chest**	Read an extract from a story and answer questions about it. Write what you think may happen next and imagine how you would behave in a similar situation. Practise using commas, and look at words that are not used any more.	To develop your skills as a reader and writer. To learn more about commas, and to extend your vocabulary.
73–75	**'Bulk of treasure here'**	Read the next part of the story and answer questions about it to see how well you read it.	To improve your ability to read in detail.
76–77	**The hunt upon the island**	Think about the characters you have already read about. Make a rough sketch map of how you think the island looks. Write a continuation of the story.	To develop your ability to plan and then write a story.
78	**Past, present, future**	Learn about time and tense.	To extend your understanding of how English sentences work.
79	**The adjective pyramid Wordpower**	Learn about adjectives, play a language game and look again at some of the words used in the unit.	To develop your skills as a writer and to learn about adjectives. To improve your vocabulary.

Treasure Island

The novels of R.L. Stevenson

Dates of publication
1883 Treasure Island
1886 Kidnapped
1886 Dr Jekyll and Mr Hyde
1888 The Black Arrow
1889 The Master of Ballantrae
1893 Catriona
1896 Weir of Hermiston (unfinished)

If you had met Robert Louis Stevenson in the late 1870s, you would probably have noticed how thin he was, how strong his voice was and how he waved his hands about. He would have been introduced to you as a writer. Writing was certainly not what his parents had planned for him. His father was an engineer and his grandfather designed lighthouses. The family pressed Robert into becoming a lawyer. Although he passed the examinations, he was not a success because his heart was not in it. He became a contributor to a variety of magazines and specialised in travel writing. His first book was about his experiences in paddling a canoe through Belgium! Five years later he published the first of his novels, Treasure Island. *It tells the story of Jim Hawkins.*

Do you know?

1 What did Robert Louis Stevenson do before becoming a writer?
2 Which novel did he publish in 1888?
3 Where did he travel by canoe?
4 What did his grandfather do?

Strange arrival

Jim Hawkins lived at The Admiral Benbow, an inn kept by his family. The story begins with the arrival of a sea captain at the inn. At least, Jim *thinks* he is a sea captain.

I remember it as if it were yesterday, as he came plodding to the inn door, his sea-chest following behind him in a hand barrow; a tall, strong, heavy, nut-brown man; his tarry pigtail falling over the shoulders of his soiled blue coat; his hands ragged and scarred, with black, broken nails; and the sabre cut across one cheek, a dirty livid white.

The picture in the words

TF

Robert Louis Stevenson could have described the arrival of the person at The Admiral Benbow in a single sentence. It might have said simply:

I remember the sailor arriving at our door.

Look at how much more of a picture he actually provides. Copy and complete this form.

How does the person walk?	
What about height?	
What size is he?	
What about skin colour?	
What colour is his hair?	
What are his clothes like?	
What are his hands like?	
Does he have any special features?	

Writing

- Now that you've filled in this chart for the sailor that Jim Hawkins remembers, create one for a person you know well.
- When you have done that, write a paragraph about the person you know entering a room.

The key to the chest

The captain takes a liking to Jim and promises him regular pocket
money if he will keep a look out for a one-legged sailor. In spite of their
friendship, there is something haunting about the captain. Other people at
the inn are frightened too, especially by his stories of life at sea. After the
captain has been visited by someone whom he calls Black Dog, he has a
stroke from which he never properly recovers. In his illness, he tells Jim
about how he is being hunted for his old sea-chest. When the captain
dies, Jim and his mother look for the key to the sea-chest.

I felt in his pockets, one after another. A few small coins, a
thimble, and some thread and big needles, a piece of pigtail
tobacco bitten away at the end, his gully with the crooked
handle, a pocket compass, and a tinder box, were all that
they contained, and I began to despair.

    'Perhaps it's round his neck,' suggested my
mother.

    Overcoming a strong repugnance, I tore open
his shirt at the neck, and there, sure enough,
10 hanging to a bit of tarry string, which I cut
with his own gully, we found the key. At this
triumph we were filled with hope, and hurried
upstairs, without delay, to the little room where he had
slept so long, and where his box had stood since the day of his
arrival.

    It was like any other seaman's chest on the outside, the initial
'B' burned on the top of it with a hot iron, and the corners
somewhat smashed and broken as by long, rough usage.

    'Give me the key,' said my mother; and though the
20 lock was very stiff, she had turned it and thrown
back the lid in a twinkling.

gully: knife

A strong smell of tobacco and tar rose from the interior but nothing
was to be seen on the top except a suit of very good clothes, carefully
brushed and folded. They had never been worn, my mother said. Under
that, the miscellany began – a quadrant, a tin canikin, several sticks of
tobacco, two brace of very handsome pistols, a piece of bar silver, an old
Spanish watch and some other trinkets of little value and mostly of
foreign make, a pair of compasses mounted with brass, and five or six
curious West Indian shells. It has often set me thinking since that he
should have carried about these shells with him in his wandering, guilty,
and hunted life.

In the meantime, we had found nothing of any value but the silver
and the trinkets, and neither of these were in our way. Underneath there
was an old boat-cloak whitened with sea-salt on many a harbour-bar. My
mother pulled it up with impatience, and there lay before us, the last
things in the chest, a bundle tied up in oilcloth, and looking like papers,
and a canvas bag, that gave forth, at a touch, the jingle of gold.

'I'll show these rogues that I'm an honest woman,' said my mother.
'I'll have my dues and not a farthing over. Hold Mrs Crossley's bag.' And
she began to count over the amount of the captain's score from the
sailor's bag into the one I was holding.

It was a long, difficult business, for the coins were of all countries and sizes – doubloons, and louis d'ors, and guineas, and pieces of eight, and I knew not what besides, all shaken together at random. The guineas, too, were about the scarcest, and it was with these only that my mother knew how to make her count.

When we were about half way through, I suddenly put my hand upon her arm; for I had heard in the silent, frosty air, a sound that brought my heart into my mouth – the tapping of the blind man's stick upon the frozen road. It drew nearer and nearer, while we sat holding our breath. Then it struck sharp on the inn door, and then we could hear the handle being turned, and the bolt rattling...

What happens next?

- Who could be at the door?
- What might that person/those people want?
- What could Jim and his mother do?

1 In the pocket

Make a chart of what Jim finds in the captain's pockets. On the left hand side write what Jim finds. On the right hand side write what you think you learn about the captain.

What Jim finds	What I learn
a few small coins	either he is poor or he does not carry much money on him

2 Inside the chest

What do the contents of the chest tell you about the captain?

1 Make a list of what Jim and his mother find.
2 Pick out two things from the chest which you are not surprised that they found. What do they tell you about the captain?
3 Pick out two things that are more puzzling. What possible explanations can you suggest for them?

3 Your own trunk

If you were keeping just five or six things in a small trunk to travel around with you, what would you choose, and why?

4 Writing

Imagine you are staying at the house of a very old relative or friend and they give you the key to a trunk in the attic. What do you find? What do you ask them about what you find? Tell the story of what happens.

Commas in lists

When you are writing a list of things in a sentence, you need to separate one item from another. This is done with commas. Here is part of the list of things Jim found in the chest:

several sticks of tobacco, two brace of very handsome pistols, a piece of bar silver, an old Spanish watch

Check that your list of things for your own small trunk has commas to separate the items in the list.

TF

Practice

Write a sentence to describe each of these:

- five items you were sent to buy from the nearest shop
- five items that were found by a teacher in an old desk
- five items that were left on the floor of the canteen at the end of the lunch break
- five items that your family left behind when they went on a trip
- five items that were found in someone's luggage when it was checked at Customs.

Old and new

Robert Louis Stevenson published this story in 1883. Some of the words he chose are not often used today. Look at two of the things found in the captain's chest:

a pair of compasses
two brace of very handsome pistols.

The words **pair** and **brace** mean the same thing but one of them is rarely used today.

- What other words can you think of meaning 'two'?
- What words can you think of for other numbers?
- Divide your words into those you would use as part of Standard English and those which belong to a particular dialect.

The money that Jim finds comes from all parts of the world and his mother only knows the value of the **guineas**. What other coins do they find?

There are literally hundreds of words for money and for particular coins or notes. How many do you know?

Create a list of words for money in three columns showing those that are used in Standard English, those that are old-fashioned and those that are used in regional dialects. (Some words will appear in two columns because they are old-fashioned *and* belong to a regional dialect.)

Standard English	Old-fashioned	Dialect
pound	sovereign	quid

'Bulk of treasure here'

The gold that Jim and his mother find may meet the captain's unpaid bills at the inn but it is the bundle tied in oilcloth that proves to be more interesting in the long run. They open it after Jim and his mother have taken shelter at Doctor Livesey's house.

The bundle was sewn together, and the doctor had to get out his instrument case, and cut the stitches with his medical scissors. It contained two things – a book and a sealed paper.

'First of all we'll try the book,' observed the doctor.

The squire and I were both peering over his shoulder as he opened it, for Dr Livesey had kindly motioned me to come round from the side-table, where I had been eating, to enjoy the sport of the search. On the first page there were only some scraps of writing, such as a man with a pen in his hand might make for idleness or practice. One was the same as the tattoo mark, 'Billy Bones his fancy'; then there was 'Mr W. Bones, mate'. 'No more rum.' 'Off Palm Key he got itt'; and some other snatches, mostly single words and unintelligible. I could not help wondering who it was that had 'got itt', and what 'itt' was that he got. A knife in his back as like as not

10

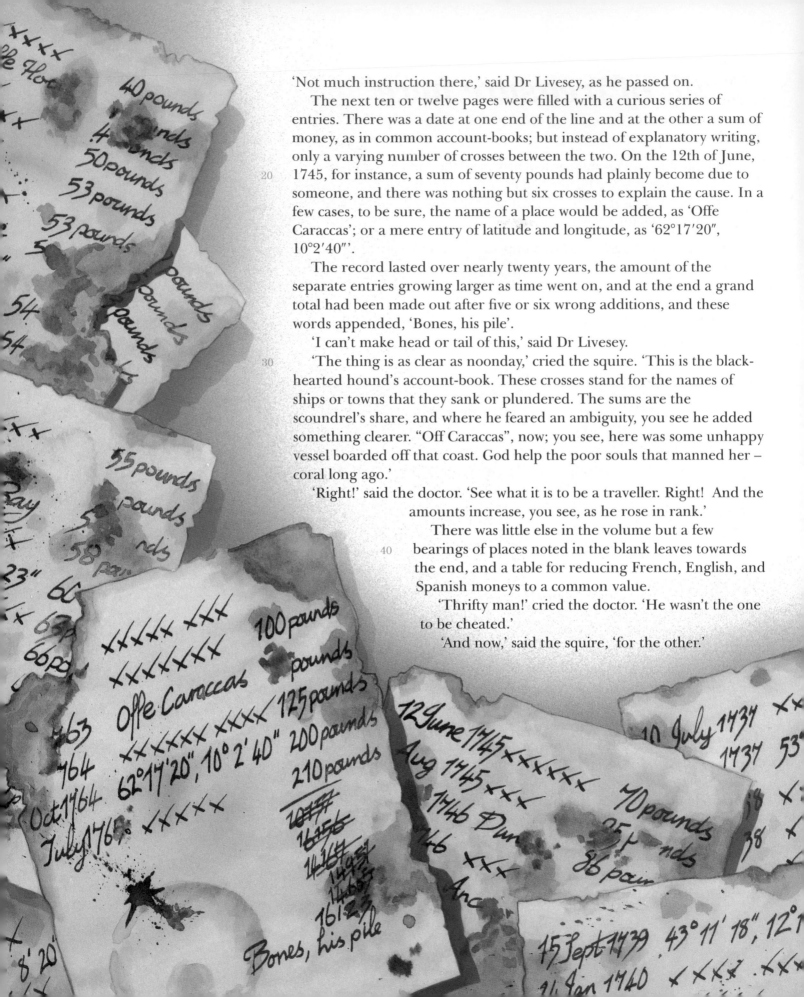

'Not much instruction there,' said Dr Livesey, as he passed on.

The next ten or twelve pages were filled with a curious series of entries. There was a date at one end of the line and at the other a sum of money, as in common account-books; but instead of explanatory writing, only a varying number of crosses between the two. On the 12th of June, 1745, for instance, a sum of seventy pounds had plainly become due to someone, and there was nothing but six crosses to explain the cause. In a few cases, to be sure, the name of a place would be added, as 'Offe Caraccas'; or a mere entry of latitude and longitude, as '62°17'20", 10°2'40"'.

The record lasted over nearly twenty years, the amount of the separate entries growing larger as time went on, and at the end a grand total had been made out after five or six wrong additions, and these words appended, 'Bones, his pile'.

'I can't make head or tail of this,' said Dr Livesey.

'The thing is as clear as noonday,' cried the squire. 'This is the black-hearted hound's account-book. These crosses stand for the names of ships or towns that they sank or plundered. The sums are the scoundrel's share, and where he feared an ambiguity, you see he added something clearer. "Off Caraccas", now; you see, here was some unhappy vessel boarded off that coast. God help the poor souls that manned her – coral long ago.'

'Right!' said the doctor. 'See what it is to be a traveller. Right! And the amounts increase, you see, as he rose in rank.'

There was little else in the volume but a few bearings of places noted in the blank leaves towards the end, and a table for reducing French, English, and Spanish moneys to a common value.

'Thrifty man!' cried the doctor. 'He wasn't the one to be cheated.'

'And now,' said the squire, 'for the other.'

The paper had been sealed in several places with a thimble by way of seal; the very thimble, perhaps, that I had found in the captain's pocket. The doctor opened the seals with great care, and there fell out the map of an island, with latitude and longitude, soundings, names of hills, and bays and inlets, and every
50 particular that would be needed to bring a ship to safe anchorage upon its shores. It was about nine miles long and five across, shaped, you might say, like a fat dragon standing up, and had two fine land-locked harbours, and a hill in the centre part marked, 'The Spy-glass'. There were several additions of a later date; but, above all, three crosses of red ink – two on the north part of the island, one in the south-west, and beside this last, in the same red ink, and in a small, neat hand, very different from the captain's tottery characters, these words: 'Bulk of treasure here.'

Over on the back the same hand had written this further information:

'Tall tree, Spy-glass shoulder, bearing a point to the N. of NNE.

60 'Skeleton Island ESE and by E.

'Ten feet.

'The bar silver is in the north cache; you can find it by the trend of the east hummock, ten fathoms south of the black crag with the face on it.

'The arms are easy found, in the sand hill, N. point of north inlet cape, bearing E. and a quarter N.

'J.F.'

That was all; but brief as it was, and, to me, incomprehensible, it filled the squire and Dr Livesey with delight.

'Livesey,' said the squire, 'you will give up this wretched practice at once.
70 Tomorrow I start for Bristol. In three weeks' time – three weeks! – two weeks – ten days – we'll have the best ship, sir, and the choicest crew in England.'

Robert Louis Stevenson: *Treasure Island*

How well did you read?

1 What did the oilcloth bundle have in it?
2 What had Jim been doing before he started to watch the bundle being untied?
3 The book appears to be a kind of diary or journal. What period of time does it cover?
4 What had the captain been doing in his book?
5 Why do the individual sums of money recorded in the captain's book get bigger as time goes by?
6 How had the captain kept the map safe?
7 How many harbours did the island on the map have?
8 How wide is the island?
9 What do the three crosses on the map appear to mark?
10 What clues do you get about the characters of Dr Livesey and the squire?

The hunt upon the island

You are going to write what you think
might happen in the hunt for the treasure.

First Think about your characters and imagine what
they are like. There are three characters here:
Jim Hawkins, Doctor Livesey and Squire
Trelawney.

**Describe what you think they might
look like and decide what they might be
like as people.**

To help you make up your mind, there are
two character wheels to look at and
illustrations of clothes from the 1750s.

Use these but add as many thoughts and
ideas of your own as you can.

Second Think about the kind of people they might
meet in their search for the treasure. By this
stage in the story we already know that other
pirates are after the treasure but they don't
have the map.

**Prepare descriptions for two of the
pirates and give them names.**

Use the illustrations and the character
wheels again to help you.

Third Decide what the island looks like. There are
some clues in the story but you will need to
add ideas of your own.

**Make a rough sketch map of the island
to help you imagine it.**

Look back at the description of the island at
the top of page 75.

Character wheel – appearance
Use this to help you think about what the people in your story might look and sound like.

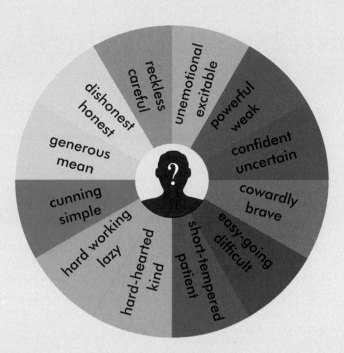

Character wheel – personality
Use this to help you think about what the people in your story might be like.

Fourth **Decide what happens on the island and what happens with the treasure.**

- Is it still there?
- Who finds the treasure or finds it is missing?
- How might the treasure be transported?
- Are there arguments?
- Are there any ambushes?
- Is the treasure recovered safely?

Finally **Decide which would be the most exciting part of the story to tell.**
Choose a title and write that part.

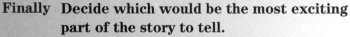
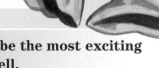

Verbs and stories

When you are telling a story, getting the verbs right is important. You can find a reminder about using verbs on page 78.

Past, present, future

Past	Present	Future
This story happened long, long ago in the past.	I am writing it now, at this very moment.	I hope you will read it soon.

Showing time

When you write a story you have two ways of showing when it happened:

- using **time words**: *Yesterday a very strange thing happened to me.*
- changing the **tense** of the verb: *Yesterday a very strange thing **happened** to me.*

Tense

Verbs have different forms for the present and the past. These forms are called tenses:

Present tense	Past tense
I walk	I walked
she walks	she walked
I go	I went
she goes	she went

When you are actually writing your story, it is sometimes easy to become confused about what tense you should use. It is easy to make this kind of mistake:

> It was getting dark. I slipped out of the house and walked quietly towards the church. In our village there is a big church with a large churchyard. I **make** my way along the side of the churchyard and **find** the gate.

The last sentence should, of course, be:

> I **made** my way along the side of the churchyard and **found** the gate.

The past

Stories are normally written using past tenses:

> Saturday afternoon **was** hot and dull. The sky **was curdled** with clouds as grey and lumpy as porridge. Anna **sat** on a high stool in the wool shop, staring through the window at the people passing by outside.

The adjective pyramid

Adjectives are sometimes seen as words which help to build a picture.

Jim Hawkins tells of the arrival of the sea captain at the inn. His description helps to answer possible questions about what the captain looks like.

He is	*a man*
and his height?	*a **tall** man*
and his build?	*a tall, **strong** man*
and his weight?	*a tall, strong, **heavy** man*
and his skin?	*a tall, strong, heavy, **nut-brown** man*

> Each adjective adds a little more to the picture of the sea captain as he trudges up to the inn door.

A language game

You can play a game in a circle where you describe someone or something and everyone has to add an extra adjective to the description without missing out any earlier ones. If you can't add an adjective or if you miss one, you're out or you lose a life.

a teacher
*a **terrific** teacher*
*a terrific, **sympathetic** teacher*
*a terrific, sympathetic, **helpful** teacher*
*a terrific, sympathetic, helpful, **intelligent** teacher*
*a terrific, sympathetic, helpful, intelligent, **imaginary** teacher*

Wordpower

All these words are in the unit you have been reading.

1 Explain the meaning of as many as you can.
2 For those you cannot explain, find them in the unit and try to work out their meaning from the sentence they are in.
3 For any that are left, look them up in a dictionary.
4 Make sure you can spell them all.

> **Pyramid starters**
> a girl
> a boy
> a man
> a woman
> a mother
> a father
> a brother
> a sister
> a dog
> a cat
> a gerbil
> a goldfish
> a nurse
> a doctor
> a policewoman

word	page	line	word	page	line	word	page	line
initial	69	16	interior	70	22	repugnance	69	8
usage	69	18	trinkets	70	27	miscellany	70	25
except	70	23	impatience	70	35	unintelligible	73	12
foreign	70	28	peering	73	5	explanatory	74	18
instrument	73	2	plundered	74	32	appended	74	28
scoundrel	74	33	thrifty	74	43	ambiguity	74	33
vessel	74	35	practice	75	69	incomprehensible	75	67

ISLANDS IN THE SUN

Between Spain and North Africa are four very popular holiday islands. The largest of these is Mallorca. The next few pages will give you the chance to discover something about this island before you take up the role of holiday guide.

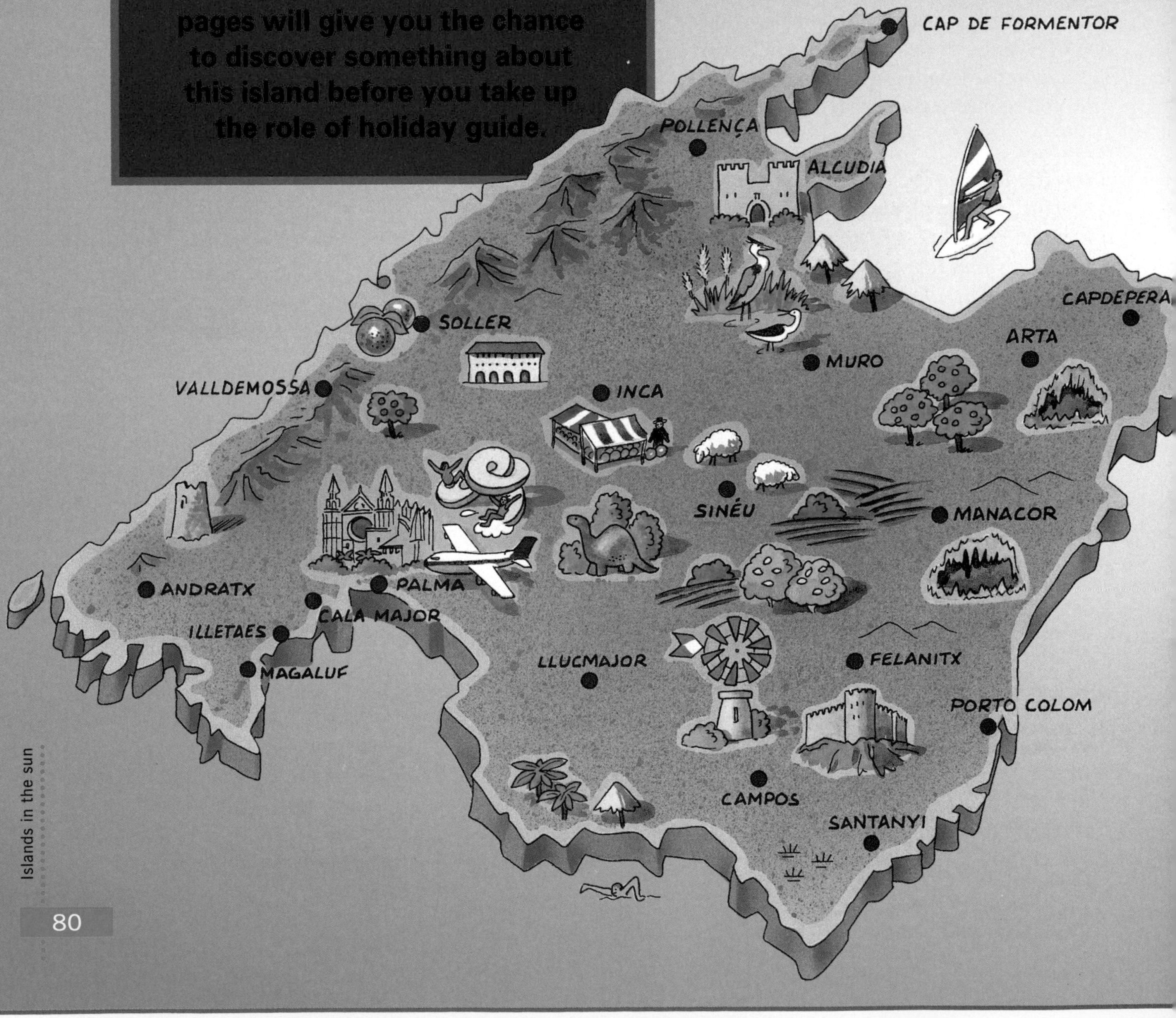

CAP DE FORMENTOR

POLLENÇA

ALCUDIA

CAPDEPERA

ARTA

SOLLER

MURO

VALLDEMOSSA

INCA

MANACOR

SINÉU

ANDRATX

PALMA

CALA MAJOR

FELANITX

ILLETAES

LLUCMAJOR

MAGALUF

PORTO COLOM

CAMPOS

SANTANYI

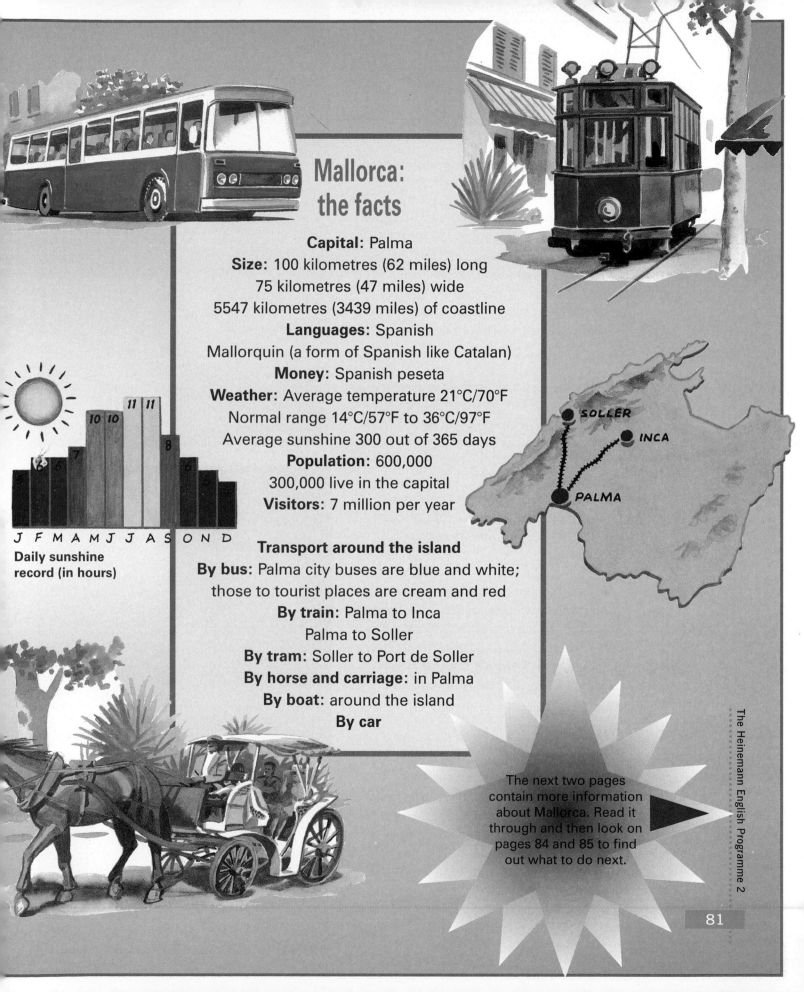

Mallorca: the facts

Capital: Palma
Size: 100 kilometres (62 miles) long
75 kilometres (47 miles) wide
5547 kilometres (3439 miles) of coastline
Languages: Spanish
Mallorquin (a form of Spanish like Catalan)
Money: Spanish peseta
Weather: Average temperature 21°C/70°F
Normal range 14°C/57°F to 36°C/97°F
Average sunshine 300 out of 365 days
Population: 600,000
300,000 live in the capital
Visitors: 7 million per year

Transport around the island
By bus: Palma city buses are blue and white;
those to tourist places are cream and red
By train: Palma to Inca
Palma to Soller
By tram: Soller to Port de Soller
By horse and carriage: in Palma
By boat: around the island
By car

Daily sunshine
record (in hours)

11 11
10 10
8
7
6 6 6 6
5 5 4

J F M A M J J A S O N D

SOLLER
INCA
PALMA

The next two pages
contain more information
about Mallorca. Read it
through and then look on
pages 84 and 85 to find
out what to do next.

The Heinemann English Programme 2

FROM ARTA ...

The Caves of Arta These caves were originally used by pirates because they overlook the sea. These days a guide will lead you through them. The stalactites and stalagmites are lit by a laser show. The largest stalagmite is 22 metres (72 feet) tall.

Marineland Here you can feed the sea lions, watch the sharks and go to the dolphin show. There are picnic areas, a small zoo, an aquarium, a playground and a beach. A ten minute bus ride from *Palma*.

Auto Safari Park The animals in the park near *Porto Cristo* are mainly African – zebras, elephants, baboons, antelopes, giraffes and many others. You don't need a car because you can tour the park by bus.

The Glassblowers of Gordiola Here you can watch as glass is blown into vases, into glasses and into animal shapes. *Gordiola* is between *Palma* and *Manacor*.

Sa Granja An old mansion which houses a museum showing how people in *Mallorca* used to live. As well as the house there are beautiful shady gardens with fountains and natural springs. There are special activities on Wednesday and Friday afternoons. These include craft skills, local food and traditional dancing.

Prehistoric Park The park, which is between *Palma* and *Manacor*, has thirty life-size dinosaur models.

Bellver Castle This castle was built in *Palma* during the fourteenth century and is unusual because it is completely round. It is also well-known for its white walls and its dungeons. If you look closely you can still see the names that the prisoners scratched on their cell walls.

... TO S'ALBUFERA

Sea and sand Mallorca has plenty of fine beaches. The longest beach is on the Bay of Alcudia. The sand stretches for 12 kilometres (7.5 miles) and the beach shelves gently so the water is shallow and safe for bathing. And if you don't feel like swimming, there are always windsurfing and pedal-boating.

Fishing There is plenty of opportunity for fishing both from the rocks and by joining a boat trip.

Aquapark This water park at *Magaluf* has kamikaze slides and a circular wave pool. There is also a small pool with little slides for younger children. In addition, the park has a children's playground, restaurants and cafes. It is well served by bus routes.

Mountain walking For those who want a change from the beaches, there are two major mountain ranges. The peaks of the *Sierra de Tramuntana* rise to over one thousand metres. You'll get peace and quiet, and cooler, fresher air...but make sure your leg muscles are up to it!

Shopping at the markets *Palma, Inca* and *Sineu* all have traditional open-air markets. *Inca* is famous for leather goods. *Sineu* has a livestock market involving horses, donkeys, sheep and goats. *Palma* has food markets but also has the *Rastrillo* on Saturdays. Here you can buy jewellery, pots, pans, antiques, even buttons.

Birdwatching Mallorca is a wonderful place if you want to do some birdwatching. Apart from the many birds that live on the island, it is on the migration route for many more. You might be lucky and see the largest bird in Europe – the black vulture – which is now in danger of extinction. One of the best places for birdwatching is the nature reserve at *S'Albufera* which is open from 9am–7pm each day.

WHERE TO STAY

HOTEL CAPRI

A small and friendly hotel in the centre of one of Mallorca's liveliest resorts. Capri is handy for the shops and bars of Puerto Pollensa.
- Pool
- Lounge with satellite TV
- Buffet or waiter-service meals
- Live music or disco every evening

HOTEL BENVENIDA

Well-situated in its own grounds, the Benvenida is on the main road leading to the centre of the resort. Plenty of bars, restaurants and cafés within easy walking distance.
- Pool and terrace bar
- Lounges and bars with snacks available
- Restaurant with waiter sevice
- Tennis courts
- Discount on fees for local golf course

HOTEL PARIS

Right on the beach, the Paris offers wonderful views and a high standard of comfort.
- Pool with terrace
- Snack bar, lounges with satellite TV, bars
- Buffet service restaurant
- Mini-golf course and volleyball court

HOTEL OASIS

Only 200 yards from the beach with a large range of services.
- Large pool with bar, garden
- Lounges, snack bar
- Buffet service restaurant
- Entertainments every day
- Pool and playground for children
- Special meals and other facilities for children (including babysitting)

What can you find out?

Mallorca quiz

Pages 80–81

1 Name two ways by which you could travel from Ínca to Palma.
2 You want to go from Palma to the beach at Alcudia. What colour bus do you need?
3 How many days without sunshine does Mallorca get each year?
4 Which are the sunniest months in Mallorca?
5 Would you expect the temperature to reach 100°F in Mallorca? Why or why not?
6 Which country is Mallorca linked with? How do you know that?

Pages 82–83

7 Where are there life-size dinosaur models?
8 What is Sierra de Tramuntana and how big is it?
9 Where do they make glass animals?
10 If you want to find water fun for all the family, where is a good place to go?
11 What is unusual about Bellver Castle?
12 Where is there a beach over seven miles long?
13 What is the Rastrillo?
14 Where should you go if you want to find out how Mallorcans used to live?

Islands in the sun

What do you recommend?

1 Where to go

Choose two places that you would like to visit from those described on pages 82 and 83. Say why you would like to go there.

Choose two places that you think would be suitable places to visit for each of the following: (Say why you have chosen them.)

- a history teacher
- a geography teacher
- a healthy retired couple who are interested in plants and in wildlife
- a family with children aged four and seven
- a family with one child who loves animals and another child who can't stand still for two minutes.

2 What to do

- Which three activities do you think would be most popular with adults? Explain how you made your choice.
- Which three activities do you think would be most popular with young people of your age? Explain how you made your choice.
- Choose four members of your class who are as different from each other as possible. Decide which activity you think they would each enjoy. Say why you made your choices.

3 Where to stay

Which of the hotels on page 84 would be most suitable for the following holidaymakers?

- a family with very young children
- a young married couple with no children
- an older couple who like to eat and drink well
- a group of friends who are keen on outdoor activities.

Advertising Mallorca

Now you are going to produce materials to tell other people about Mallorca: TF

- a poster advertising Mallorca to families
- a one-page advertisement for one of the hotels on page 84, giving information both about the hotel and the island
- a two-page display aimed at teachers interested in Mallorca
- a short guide to Mallorca for 8–10-year-olds visiting the island for the first time. (One way to do this would be in a question-and-answer format.)

The Heinemann English Programme 2

The square-eyed monster

The square-eyed monster

The square-eyed MONSTER

You can get a university degree by using the television. You can also waste the equivalent of whole years by sitting in front of the 'box'. What do you think about television?

First thoughts

Write one or two sentences in answer to each of these questions:

1 What is your favourite kind of programme?
2 What sort of programme do you dislike?
3 What do people in your family think about television?
4 In what ways is television good for people?
5 In what ways is television bad for people?

Group discussion

Now discuss your ideas with people in your group.

The Heinemann English Programme 2

The TV kid

All that Lenny wants to do is watch television. His mother would prefer to see him busy completing his chores or doing his homework. Whatever he is supposed to be doing, there is always the terrible temptation to watch. His mother has banned all television until his grades in school improve. So, instead of watching the programmes, he dreams about them, especially the game shows.

'And now, Lennie, you have won over three thousand dollars in cash and merchandise and, more important, you have won the chance to spin our Vacation Wheel. How do you feel about that, Lennie?'

'Real good, sir.'

'Then join me over here at the Vacation Wheel. Now, Lennie, I don't have to remind you that up there on the wheel are twenty, all-expense paid vacations to places all over the world, do I?'

'No, sir.'

10 'That's twenty, all-expense paid vacations! You can go to Rome, to London, to Paris. You can go to beautiful Hawaii, exotic Mexico or sunny Spain. All in all, there are twenty, wonderful, all-expense paid vacations up there on the wheel. But, Lennie, as you know, there are also what we call our zonk trips. How do you feel about those, Lennie?'

'Well, I hope I don't get one.'

'And that's what we're hoping too, aren't we, folks? Hear that applause,
20 Lennie? They're all with you. Now step up close to the Vacation Wheel. That's right. The three zonk trips, as we call them, are here and here and here. Try not to land on them.'

'I will, sir.'

'All right, put up your hand now, Lennie, right here on the Vacation Wheel, and Lennie, give it a spin!'

'Here goes!'

'Good boy! The wheel is spinning, folks. Lennie really gave it a good spin, didn't he? Where do you want to go, Lennie?'

'Any of those places is all right with me.'

'Except the zonk places, right?'

'Right.'

'It's still spinning, and now it's beginning to slow down. Watch the wheel, folks. Where is Lennie going? To Paris? Rome? London? It's almost stopped. It looks like Egypt! No! Rio! No! Oh, no! Look at that! Lennie, you have landed on number thirteen, one of our zonk trips, and I don't have to tell you what that means.'

'It means I'm going to have to take a zonk trip.'

'Right.'

'Where?'

'Well, let me look in my zonk envelope. Oh, Lennie.'

'What?'

'Oh, Lennie.'

'What? What is it?'

'Oh, Lennie!'

'What? I want to know. What is it?'

'Lennie, you are going to have to spend one full night, all-expense paid, in a haunted house!'

'A what?'

'Yes, Lennie, you heard correctly, you are going to Haunted House Number Thirteen located right on the outskirts – that's the dark, scary outskirts, I might add – of beautiful downtown –'

'But I don't want to spend the night in any haunted house.'

'Of course you don't, but you take your chances, Lennie, just like all the other contestants. Remember that paper you signed when you came on the show?'

'Yes, but I didn't – I mean I couldn't – I mean –'

'Oh, all right, Lennie, I'll tell you what I'm going to do. You go to the haunted house, spend one night there, and if you survive – I say, if you survive – then you come back next week and we'll let you spin the Vacation Wheel again. How about that?'

'But, sir, couldn't I just take my three thousand in cash and merchandise and –'

'How many want to see him take the cash and merchandise and go home?'

Silence.

'How many want to see him go to the haunted house?'

Wild applause.

'But, sir –'

'See, the audience is with you. Hear that applause? Well, it's time for a commercial break now, but stay with us, folks, for the second half of Give it a Spin, the show where you pick your prizes and we see that you take them.'

Betsy Byars: *The TV kid*

Thinking about game shows

TF

1 List as many game shows as you can.
2 Which are the best? Which are the worst? Why?
3 Think about one game show.

- How does it work?
- What is the scoring system?
- How do you win?
- What are the prizes?

4 Think about a different game show.

- Which things are similar to the first show you looked at?
- Which things are different?

The square-eyed monster

Create your own game show

If you are going to create a game show, there is a lot to discuss and decide. Discuss each of the topics listed. Decide what *your* game show will be like. Make sure that, at each stage, someone in your group writes down what you have decided. Then, when you have finished, you can describe your show to the rest of the class.

1 What is the basic idea?

- Shows can be based on a sport.
- Shows can be based on a subject.
- Shows can be based on a word game.
- Shows can be based around famous people.
- Shows can be totally new and not based on any of these things.

2 What questions will you ask?

- You will need a good supply of questions.
- Do you need them at several levels of difficulty?

3 What is the scoring system?

- The simplest is a points system.
- Many shows base their scoring on a well-known game (for example: darts, snakes and ladders, noughts and crosses, snooker or tennis).
- You can also have people collecting letters to make up words.

4 Who will take part?

- Individuals or teams?
- Celebrities?
- Ordinary people?
- Celebrities partnering ordinary people?

5 Who will run the show (the 'host' or 'hostess')?

- Does he or she need assistants?
- Do you need any resident experts?

6 What are the prizes?

- Most shows have a range of prizes.
- What will be the top prize?
- What will the other prizes be?
- Will there be booby prizes like the zonk trips?

7 What will the show be called?

- The name needs to be short and snappy.
- It also needs to suggest what kind of show it is.

The country boy

Bernard Ashley is best known for his novels such as *A kind of wild justice* and *Bad blood*. After two of his novels – *Break in the sun* and *Running scared* – had been televised, he became involved in a project that was planned as a television series from the start.

The story develops from something that happens at the end of the first episode. Here are the final scenes of that episode.

Characters
Tony
Sally
Baz
Div
Pilk
West
Dr Skellman

1 Footpath to J.M. Chemicals (UK) Ltd
(*Sally is coming down the track from where the bus dropped her. Her face lights up as she sees someone coming. We see Tony approaching on his bike.*)

SALLY: Watch out!

(*Tony cycles up to her. She holds his handlebars.*)

10

TONY: Watch out for what?
SALLY: You could've come off.

(*Sally lets go of his handlebars and he does a long controlled wobble, straight at her. She jumps back.*)

SALLY: Watch out!
TONY: Perfect control. Was your bus late?
SALLY: A bit. (*Stares at him innocently.*) Slow getting away. (*They start to walk off.*) And I mustn't be too long.

2 Bank of the inlet – near the Old Customs Houses

20 (*Tony and Sally come in through some bushes.*)

TONY: Wanna swim?

(*Sally stares at him. This has implications.*)

SALLY: (*Breaks the mood.*) My dad'd kill me if I went in there.

TONY: Why? Is it dangerous?

SALLY: He reckons. River comes in, currents. He's real strict about it.

(*Tony puts his hand up to her to sit down, but we hear the sound of the bikers approaching.*)

30 SALLY: Oh, no!

TONY: Them again!

SALLY: Come on.

(*They run out onto the road to be in the open when the bikers get there.*)

3 The inlet

(*The three bikers come along the track to the Customs Houses, forming into a circle around Sally and Tony, who try to look tolerantly amused. This mustn't be too menacing, the ad libs more to*
40 *do with biking skill than menace.*)

4 The Old Customs Houses

(*They park up their bikes.*)

BAZ: 'Old on! Gotta go somewhere.

OTHERS: Yeah! Yeah!

(*Baz runs to the house Brit and Scot have been in. We hear splintering wood.*)

DIV: What we gonna do?

PILK: You busted all the windows.

(*Baz opens the upstairs windows of the house.*)

50 BAZ: 'Ere, look! (*He lifts a canister in his hands.*) Targets!

DIV: Better than nothing.

BAZ: Some old farmer's fertilizer! (*Slings it down from window.*)

Questions

1 In what kind of place is this scene set?

2 What do we learn about Sally and Tony from the scene?

tolerantly amused
    Sally and Tony try to pretend that they are putting up with it and find it slightly funny in a childish sort of way

ad libs
    words spoken by the actors in performance but not written down in the script

Questions

3 Who are Baz, Div, and Pilk?

4 What are your first impressions of them?

5 How do Sally and Tony react to them?

6 How do they treat Sally and Tony?

5 Bank of the inlet

(*The canister is standing on a post at the inlet's edge. The three youths are throwing flints at it. Div takes aim. He just pings it.*)

PILK: Only clipped it.
60 DIV: Rotten shot.

(*Pilk throws. There is a dull clunk.*)

PILK: Boom! Oh, yes!
DIV: Smackeroo!
BAZ: (*Picks up a bigger flint.*) Watch this! Top third, in the 'ead, smack it over. (*He takes very careful aim, throws, misses.*)
PILK: Yah! Missed it!
DIV: Oh, smack it over! Wallie!

(*Baz, enraged, jumps up, runs to the canister and*
70 *throws it into the inlet.*)

BAZ: Smack in! All right?

(*Close up of the canister sinking, one small flint hole sending out a first fine curl of yellow chemical.*)

Question

7 What have the bikers done?

WEST: How's it going, Les?

DR SKELLMAN: (*Finishes making an entry.*) Did you knock? Please knock in future.

WEST: What progress? Is the stuff safe yet?

DR SKELLMAN: I could dilute it tomorrow but you want something else!

WEST: I want something cost-effective.

DR SKELLMAN: Separating molecules takes time.

WEST: Time is what we haven't got.

(*He goes quickly, without giving her the option not to reply.*)

Bernard Ashley: *The country boy*

Questions

8 What impression do you get of West?

9 And of Dr Skellman?

Acting out a scene

The best way to get to know and understand a script is to act it.

Work in a group

1 Read the whole script through.
2 Choose one of these groups of scenes:

   ■ 1 and 2
   ■ 4 and 5

3 Discuss how it should be performed. In particular, talk about:

   ■ how the characters speak and behave
   ■ what they think and feel about each other
   ■ the **pace** of the scene.

4 Cast the parts.

5 Read the script through, without moving. Just try to get the voice right.
6 Now discuss how it should be acted. Some of the movements are described in the script, but you will probably have to add details of your own.
7 Try the scene out.
8 Discuss how it went and what changes should be made to improve it.
9 Try the scene again.
10 Continue in this way until you are satisfied with your performance.

Meeting the characters

In the first episode of a series, it is important to establish basic facts about characters and to let your audience get a fair idea about what is going on. At the same time, you need some things that are mysterious or unexplained so that your audience will tune in next time.

1 What do you discover about the characters that you meet here? Make a chart with three columns. Write the characters' names in the first column and your comments in the second.
2 Look at the chart you have made. For each of the character points, find the place(s) in the script that made you think this. Write them in the third column.
3 Choose two characters. For each of them write a few sentences explaining what we have learned about them and how we have learned it. Use the information in your chart and add any extra ideas you may have.

Character	Comments
Tony	– seems keen to meet Sally
	– has met bikers before
	– isn't afraid of bikers
Sally	
Baz	

Comments	Evidence
– seems keen to meet Sally	asks her if her bus
met bikers before	was late, so he
of bikers	must have been
	wondering what had
	happened to her

Story lines

Scriptwriters produce a story line to show briefly
what is going to happen in each episode. How might
the story develop from here?

1 Think about:

- what might happen to Tony and Sally
- what the bikers might do
- what Dr Skellman is doing
- why West is in a hurry
- the possible effects of the chemical.

2 Write down your best ideas for possible story
   lines. Don't worry about working out all the details.
   Just write down the main points.

Making a scenario

3 Choose the story line you like best.
4 Think out in detail how it might develop.
5 Make a list of the main scenes and fill in the
   details, like this:

Setting:	Near the Old Customs Houses
Characters:	Tony, Sally, Baz, Div, Pilk
Actions:	Tony meets Sally but their conversation is interrupted by the arrival of the bikers, Baz, Div, and Pilk. The bikers find a canister

Writing the script

6 Choose one of your main scenes to work on.
7 Think about *exactly* what happens in it. (You may
   need to make some notes as you think about this.)
8 Write the script of your scene.

Advice

There is advice about setting out a script on page 98.

Script

On pages 92 to 95
you saw how a
script is presented
in a printed book.

> **2 *Bank of the inlet – near the Old Customs Houses***
> (*Tony and Sally come in through some bushes.*)
>
> TONY: Wanna swim?
>
> (*Sally stares at him. This has implications.*)
>
> SALLY: (*Breaks the mood.*) My dad'd kill me if I went in there.

That isn't, of course,
how Bernard Ashley
presented it to the
BBC. His version
was probably
something like this:

> 2 Bank of the inlet – near the Old Customs Houses
>
> (TONY AND SALLY COME IN THROUGH SOME BUSHES.)
> TONY: Wanna swim?
> (SALLY STARES AT HIM. THIS HAS IMPLICATIONS.)
> SALLY: (BREAKS THE MOOD.) My dad'd kill me if I went in there.

Both versions make clear differences between the main types
of information in the script:

- where the scene takes place
- descriptions of the place and what the characters do
- the characters' names
- what the characters say.

Look at both examples and see how they do this.

If you are using a word-processor you can copy either of these versions
(although the second may be easier to do). If you are using handwriting,
you can copy the second one, or use a slightly easier version:

Where the scene takes place ⟶ 2 BANK OF THE INLET – NEAR THE OLD CUSTOMS HOUSES

Descriptions and actions ⟶ (Tony and Sally come in through some bushes.)

Characters' names ⟶ TONY: Wanna swim?

What they say ⟶ (Sally stares at him. This has implications.)

SALLY: (Breaks the mood.) My dad'd kill me if I went in there.

Adverbs

How does he go?
Where does she jump?

If you study the descriptions in the script of what the characters do, you will find that the writer describes how the actions are performed:

He goes quickly.
She jumps back.

The words that do this are adverbs. Adverbs do two main jobs:

1 They work in a sentence with the verb, to tell us the answer to questions like:

- how? *He goes **quickly**.*
- where? *She jumps **back**.*
- when? ***Later** they return.*

2 They come before an adjective or another adverb and answer the question:

- how much? *He's a **strangely** ugly young man.*
  *She goes **very** quickly.*

Another clue

A large number of adverbs are formed by adding the suffix **-ly** to adjectives:

quick → quickly

So if a word ends in **-ly**, there's a good chance it is an adverb, but not always.

Wordsearch: how?

In a playscript, we are often very interested to know how characters do things.

Here is a list of adverbs describing how a person might move:

nimbly	lifelessly	restlessly
eagerly	dozily	clumsily
slyly	laboriously	effortlessly
humbly	aggressively	

1 Explain in your own words (or demonstrate!) what each of them means.
2 Add five words of your own to the list.

In the manner of the word

You can turn this into an acting game for a group or the whole class:

1 One person (the 'guesser') is chosen and leaves the room.
2 The rest of the group chooses an adverb.
3 The guesser then comes back and has to work out what the adverb is.
4 S/he does this by asking people in the group to mime actions 'in the manner of the word'. So, if the adverb is *sleepily*, the guesser might ask someone to 'eat a meal in the manner of the word'. The chosen person has to mime eating a meal *sleepily*.
5 After each mime, the guesser is allowed one guess at the adverb.
6 The game continues until the guesser works out what the adverb is.

Spelling: an ant or an ent?

In this unit, you have come across one of the words that adults spell wrongly again and again – *independent*.

The problem is the last three letters. Many people are not sure which words end in *-ent* as *independent* does and which end in *-ant*.

This exercise will help you to avoid making that sort of mistake. The list below gives you words ending in *-ent* or *-ant*. Your job is to work out what the word is and how it is spelt. The first two are done for you.

1 independent	not controlled by others	
2 entrant	a person who enters a competition	
3 abs...	not present	
4 sil...	not making a noise	
5 assist...	a person who helps those in charge	
6 inst...	immediate	
7 pati...	not short-tempered	
8 dist...	far away	
9 innoc...	not guilty	
10 dec...	proper	
11 resid...	a person who lives in a place	

12 adolesc...	teenager
13 bril.....	very bright
14 diff.....	not the same as
15 ele.....	a large animal
16 arg.....	a disagreement
17 intel......	clever
18 obed....	well-behaved
19 ign.....	not educated
20 exce.....	superb
21 acc.....	an unintended event
22 rel.....	appropriate to the subject being discussed

Extension

How many other words ending in *-ent* or *-ant* can you think of?
Compile a list and create a puzzle like the one you have just completed.

Words

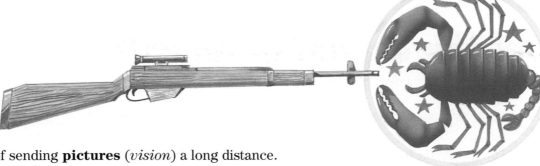

On the tele-

Television is a way of sending **pictures** (*vision*) a long distance.
A *telescope* is something that helps you **see** (*scope*) a long distance.

1 What do you think *tele-* means in those two words?
2 How many other words can you think of that begin with the letters *tele-*? Make a list of them.
3 Look at each of the words you have listed and try to break each one down as we did *television* and *telescope*.
4 What do you imagine each of these words means?

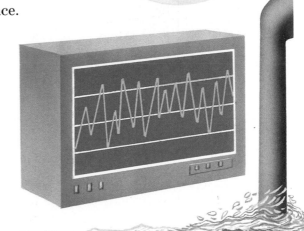

     telecommunications
     telerobot
     teleteaching

5 Now make a list of all the words you can think of that contain the letters *-scope*. Look at the pictures for clues.

Wordpower

All these words are in the unit you have been reading.

1 Explain the meanings of as many as you can.
2 For those you cannot explain, find them in the unit and try to work out their meaning from the sentence they are in. Then check them in a dictionary.
3 If there are any left, look them up in the dictionary.
4 Make sure that you can spell them.

word	page	line	word	page	line	word	page	line
expense	88	10	vacation	88	3	merchandise	88	2
beautiful	88	11	exotic	88	12	contestants	89	57
applause	88	19	outskirts	89	53	commercial	90	73
beginning	89	34	thousand	90	64	inlet	93	19
haunted	89	50	audience	90	72	implications	93	22
canister	93	50	innocently	92	16	tolerantly	93	38
			fertilizer	93	53	molecules	95	82

First things first!

Page	Title	What you do	Why you do it
103	**First things first?**	Study a picture story and predict what will happen next.	To start you thinking about the theme of the unit.
104–106	**First things first?**	Read the newspaper reports, and compare them.	To develop your close reading skills.
107–108	**Commas**	Learn about commas and understand where to use them. Practise what you have just learnt.	To improve your punctuation.
109	**Verbs: more about tenses**	Learn to identify and use verbs and tenses.	To extend your understanding of how sentences work.
110–112	**Horror film**	Read a poem aloud. Learn about the different ways people speak. Write about a film, and do a review of a play, book or film.	To improve your skills as a reader and writer. Learn how to write a review.
113	**Spelling Wordpower**	Revise spelling and look again at some of the words in the unit.	To improve your spelling and vocabulary.

First things first?

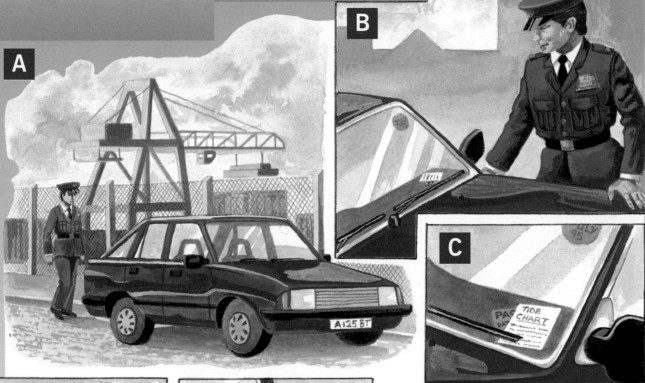

What do you think will happen next?

Why?

These are two reports that appeared in national daily newspapers. Read them both and look for the main similarities and differences.

Car clamper rises to new heights

ALAN PEARMAN, a wheelclamp official, was left dangling yesterday when he and his car were hoisted 10 feet in the air by a fork-lift truck.

It happened after Mr Pearman, 27, clamped a Saab car on Torquay harbourside belonging to a crane driver Steve Carter, 40.

Mr Carter's boss, John Thompson, hoisted Mr Pearman's Fiesta van aloft – with him inside – claiming that Mr Carter's car was parked legally in the company's parking space.

Mr Thompson said: 'I was so angry that if the forklift hadn't jammed, I'd have dumped him in the harbour.'

Mr Pearman said: 'He lifted me up twice. The first time it was about four-and-a-half feet in the air. Then he dropped the van suddenly on to the concrete on the harbourside. Then he went back a couple of feet, rammed me and lifted me up again, this time a lot higher. I don't mind telling you it was pretty frightening.'

Mike Charles, head of A1 Securities which operates the wheelclamps, said: 'It could have been very dangerous if the car had fallen off. Alan is very shaken up by it all and the car has suffered considerable damage.'

Mr Thompson was interviewed by police and told that he would not be charged.

Torquay police said the car's parking permit was partially covered by a tide table and Mr Pearman could not see the expiry date. It added: 'He phoned his boss for advice and was told to clamp the car.'

The Independent

HIGH-RISE CLAMPER

Wheel-clamper Alan Pearman was left dangling when he and his car were hoisted 10 feet in the air by a furious fork-lift truck driver yesterday. Mr Pearman, 27, immobilised a Saab car at Torquay harbour belonging to crane driver Steve Carter, 40. But Mr Carter's boss, John Thompson, thought the car was legally parked and hoisted Mr Pearman's Fiesta van aloft – with him inside.

Daily Express

The Heinemann English Programme 2

What happened when?

These reports do not begin with the first thing that happened. They start halfway through the story.

TF

1 Look at the *Daily Express* story, and then copy and complete this table:

Text	Picture letter
Wheel-clamper Alan Pearman was left dangling	J
when he and his car were hoisted 10 feet in the air by a	J
furious fork-lift truck driver yesterday.	
Mr Pearman, 27, immobilised a Saab car at Torquay harbour	
belonging to crane driver Steve Carter, 40.	
But Mr Carter's boss, John Thompson, thought the car was legally parked	
and hoisted Mr Pearman's Fiesta van aloft – with him inside.	

2 Which pictures are not described in the *Daily Express* story?
3 Now look at *The Independent* story. Use a table like this to work out the order in which the pictures come.
4 How many of the pictures are described in *The Independent* story?

Lines	Picture
1 – 4	J

5 Both versions start in the middle of the story. Why do you think they do this?

Mr Pearman's version
6 Now tell Mr Pearman's version of the story. Imagine that he gets home and tells his family what happened. Write as if you were him.

Commas

Putting things in brackets

Have you ever noticed how journalists love telling us how old people are?

They often do it in this way, putting the age after the person's name and enclosing it in commas:

Mr Pearman, 27, immobilised a SAAB car.

This is like putting it in brackets:

Mr Pearman (27) immobilised a SAAB car.

Later in the same story we read:

But Mr Carter's boss, John Thompson, thought the car was legally parked.

We use commas like this to add extra information which is useful, but not essential to the sentence: you can leave the words out and the sentence still makes good sense.

But Mr Carter's boss thought the car was legally parked.

You can do the same thing using dashes instead of commas:

Mr Carter's boss, John Thompson, hoisted Mr Pearman's Fiesta van aloft – with him inside – claiming that...

Advice

Always use two
Remember that if you use brackets, you always have to use two. This also applies if you use commas or dashes to do the same job.

Don't do it too often
If you use this way of writing too often, it can become irritating or even confusing for the reader. Look at this passage. How would you rewrite it to improve it?

I met Jonty one day last week – Thursday I think it was – while I was going along the High Street (just outside W.H. Smiths, to be precise) on my way to buy a CD. Jonty says that she's planning to go to Pembroke some time next week, probably on Thursday or Friday, because she has a friend – called Shaun, I think – with a caravan on a site, somewhere near Saundersfoot, which he says that Jonty can borrow.

Revision: using commas

Commas are used:

- to put things 'in brackets'

- to separate the items in a list:

  He turned out his pockets and found:
  a battery, a broken penknife, a lucky
  stone, and some chewing gum.

- with direct speech:

  Then he said, 'Just forget it.'

- to mark a pause between two sections in a
  sentence:

  If something isn't done soon, we shall be
  in serious trouble.

Practice

Copy out this story, putting in commas
where they are needed.

Four teenage joyriders were injured one
seriously when their car crashed and
overturned at an accident black spot last
night.

The youngsters two youths and two girls
believed to be aged 14–16 had to be cut free
from the wreckage by fire crews. They were
immediately taken to hospital.

The accident occurred at the notorious
Horseshoe Corner on the A1078 at about
9pm.

Police who were quickly at the scene have
not released the identities of the injured
teenagers.

One of the youths believed to have been
the driver of the stolen car received internal
injuries and head wounds while the others
escaped with relatively minor injuries.

A spokesman at Brumsgrove General
Hospital told the *West Midlands Times* all
four were in a 'satisfactory' condition this
morning.

He said 'The youngsters were very lucky.
If the emergency services had not been at
the scene so quickly to treat them their
injuries might have been more complicated.'

Detectives believe the car was stolen
locally last night although it is registered in
the southeast.

Horseshoe Corner a mile and a half east
of Helperton on the Brumsgrove to
Yedingville road has long been an accident
black spot.

Verbs: more about tenses

The two newspaper stories on page 105 are told mainly in the past tense:

*Wheel-clamper Alan Pearman who **was** left dangling...*

Look at the extract from the *Daily Express* on page 105. Find three verbs in the past tense.

Need to check?
If you aren't sure about this, look back to page 78 for more information about the past tense.

Mixing your tenses

When you are telling a story you should normally stick to the past tense. There are two forms of this:

> ## As I **was walking** to school I **met** Dave.
>
> | This is called the **past continuous.** We use it for actions that go on (continue) for a period of time. | This is the **simple past**. We use it mainly for simple completed actions. |
> | --- | --- |

Think of a verb

The verbs in this text have been missed out. Think of a suitable verb to fill each space. Then copy and complete the table below.

It ——(1) a long hot Saturday in June when Julie first ——(2) that there ——(3) something wrong in the house. She ——(4) in the garden at the time. She ——(5) a story for her English homework when she suddenly ——(6) a strange noise. She ——(7) carefully: there ——(8) definitely a sound of crackling. She ——(9) towards the house. All at once there ——(10) a loud bang and flames ——(11) out of the kitchen window.

A	B	C	D
Space	Verb	Correct form	Tense
1	be	was	simple past

Write on

1 Now tell the rest of the story.
2 When you have finished, underline the verb phrases.
3 Write down the first five verbs you used.
4 Against each one write as many verbs as you can think of that have similar meanings, for example:

   Ran: hurried,   rushed,
              charged,   hurtled

5 Underline the one that you think is best for your story.
6 Now do the same for the rest of the verbs you have used.

The Heinemann English Programme 2

Horror film

Well sir, first of all there was this monster
But like he's not really a monster
'Cause in real life he's a bank clerk sir
And sings in this village choir
But he keeps like drinking this potion sir
And you see him like changing into this pig
With black curly hairs on its knuckles;
And what he does sir,
Is he goes round eating people's brains.
10   Anyway before that sir, I should have said
He's secretly in love with Lady Irene
Who's very rich with lots of long frocks
And she has this identical twin sister
Who looks like her sir
Who keeps getting chased by this monster bulldog
Into these sinking sands
That's inhabited by this prehistoric squid sir
Which like she can't see
Because the deaf and dumb bailiff
20   With the hump on his back

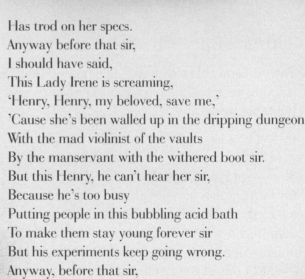

Has trod on her specs.
Anyway before that sir,
I should have said,
This Lady Irene is screaming,
'Henry, Henry, my beloved, save me,'
'Cause she's been walled up in the dripping dungeon
With the mad violinist of the vaults
By the manservant with the withered boot sir.
But this Henry, he can't hear her sir,
30   Because he's too busy
Putting people in this bubbling acid bath
To make them stay young forever sir
But his experiments keep going wrong.
Anyway, before that sir,

I should have said,
Her Dad can't rescue her either sir
Because of the army of giant ants
That's eating his castle;
And the music sir, it's going,
40   'Tarrar, tarrar, boom boom tarrar' sir,
And 'Henry, Henry my beloved,'
She keeps screaming
And the mad violinist of the vaults sir
He starts going funny all over the flagstones.
And like, Algernon sir,
No not him sir, the other one,
He can't do nothing about the squid in the bogs
Because he's turning into this pig with hairy knuckles.
Anyway before that sir, I should have said,
50   There's this huge mummy in the library
And every time he hears this music
Starts tearing off all these dirty bandages
And smashing through these walls and everything
And the professor can't stop him
'Cause he's gone off his rocker
And keeps bulging his eyes and laughing a lot

When suddenly this vampire.
Didn't I tell you about the vampire sir?
Anyway before that there's this vampire
60   Who's been dead for thousands of years
But he's a Swiss greengrocer in real life
But the iceberg his coffin's in
Gets all broken up sir
When it collides with Dr Strenkhoff's submarine sir,
That's carrying this secret cargo
Of radioactive rats.
Didn't I tell you about the radioactive rats sir?
Well anyway sir
Before that I should have said...

Gareth Owen

1 Performance time

This is a good activity to do with a **partner** or in a **small group**: you can comment on each other's performance and make suggestions about how it could be improved.

As you read this poem you can probably 'hear' the speaker's voice. Try to reproduce it.

1 Choose a section of between five and ten lines.
2 Think carefully about how those lines should sound.
3 Practise reading them until you think you have got them 'right'.

2 What a way to talk!

TF

One of the reasons why it is easy to 'hear' the voice of the poem is that it has been written in a relaxed, slangy way. It is definitely not in Standard English. For example the speaker says, 'He can't do nothing about the squid.' In Standard English we would say, 'He can't do anything about the squid.'

- Find as many other examples of non-standard English as you can.
- For each one say what it would be in Standard English.

3 Writing about a film

Take this poem as a pattern for your own writing. Imagine that the same speaker has seen another exciting film or television programme. For example:

- a police or crime film
- an Australian or British soap
- a sci-fi film.

Choose a film or programme that you have seen yourself and describe it to 'sir' as the speaker in the poem would.

4 Writing a review

TF

When you have seen a film or play, or read a book, you might be asked to write a review of it. Normally a review contains these features:

- a summary of the story (or the contents if it is, for example, a non-fiction book)
- comments on one or two important features (for example, a description of the main character(s))
- an expression of the reviewer's opinion about it: whether s/he would recommend it to other people.

Choose a film, or play that you have seen, or a book you have read, and write a review of it.

Spelling

Revision: -ing and -ed TF

The rules

1 Normally just add the suffix:

   *walk – walk**ing** – walk**ed***

2 One syllable words with a short vowel and ending in a consonant. Double the consonant:

   *rub – rub**b**ing – rub**b**ed*
   *tap – tap**p**ing – tap**p**ed*

3 One syllable words with a long vowel and ending in an **e**. Remove the **e**:

   *rak**e** – raking – raked*
   *tap**e** – taping – taped*

4 Words ending in **l** with one vowel before it, double the **l**:

   *repel – repel**l**ing – repel**l**ed*

5 Words ending in **y** with a consonant before it, change the **y** to an **i** when you add **-ed**:

   *cry – crying – cr**i**ed*

Wordpower

All these words are in the unit you have been reading.

1 Explain the meanings of as many as you can.
2 For those you cannot explain, find them in the unit and try to work out their meaning from the sentence they are in. Then check them in a dictionary.
3 If there are any left, look them up in the dictionary.
4 Make sure you can spell them.

Try it

Copy and complete the table:

base form	+ -ing	+ -ed
beg		
dare		
coil		
cry		
rake		
fail		
compel		

Odd ones

What is the rule for these words?

lie
say (and pay and lay)
sharpen

word	page	line	word	page	line	word	page	line
wheelclamp	105	1	permit	105	36	bailiff	110	19
hoist(ed)	105	3	partial(ly)	105	36	dungeon	110	26
legal(ly)	105	12	expiry	105	38	vault(s)	110	27
harbourside	105	21	immobilise(d)	105	44	flagstone(s)	111	44
interview(ed)	105	32	aloft	105	48	radioactive	111	66
potion	110	5	prehistoric	110	17			

All in order?

Most stories tell of a series of events in the order in which they happen.
Some stories mix present and past by the use of 'flashbacks'.
Occasionally, a story will unfold by starting at the end...
In this project, you explore exactly what happened
in such a story.

West Midlands Times

Wednesday, January 3

END OF A JOYRIDE
Teenagers Crash at Accident Black Spot

END OF A JOYRIDE
Teenagers Crash at Accident Black Spot

FOUR TEENAGE JOYRIDERS were injured – one seriously – when their car crashed and overturned at an accident black spot last night.

The youngsters, two youths and two girls, believed to be aged 14–16, had to be cut free from the wreckage by fire crews. They were immediately taken to hospital.

The accident occurred at the notorious Horseshoe Corner on the A1078 at about 9pm. Police, who were quickly at the scene, have not released the identities of the injured teenagers.

One of the youths, believed to have been the driver of the stolen car, received internal injuries and head wounds, while the others escaped with relatively minor injuries.

A spokesman at Brumsgrove General Hospital told the *West Midlands Times* all four were in a 'satisfactory' condition this morning.

He said, 'The youngsters were very lucky. If the emergency services had not been at the scene so quickly to treat them, their injuries might have been more complicated.'

Detectives believe the car was stolen locally last night, although it is registered in the Southeast.

Horseshoe Corner, a mile and a half east of Helperton on the Brumsgrove to Yedingville road, has long been an accident black spot. In the last five years it has claimed 13 lives. This latest accident will no doubt lead to renewed pressure for a review of County Council policy on this stretch of road.

My story

Imagine that you are one of the young people involved.
Write your version of the evening's events.

West Midlands Times

Thursday, January 4

CRASH CAR LINKED TO ARMED ROBBERY

Local men held

A car used by four teenage joyriders on Tuesday night has been linked to an armed robbery in Sussex.

Brumsgrove detectives say they found valuable antiques in the boot of the Ford Escort after it crashed at Horseshoe Corner.

The antiques, including jewellery and silver, linked the car with an armed robbery at the home of a Sussex businessman on Tuesday evening. Three Brumsgrove men are now in custody, helping the police with their enquiries.

Strange twist

The crash car was stolen in London on Christmas Eve, and police believe it was hidden in the Brumsgrove area until used in the robbery. After the crime it was driven back up the motorway and left for a short time in a Brumsgrove side street. It was then that the teenagers took the car – before the criminals had time to dispose of the proceeds of the robbery.

It was this strange twist of fate which led police on a fruitful chain of enquiries: from motor accident to joy-riding offence to armed robbery.

All four teenagers involved in the accident are recovering in Brumsgrove General Hospital.

The plot thickens

What to do

We can assume that the armed robbers quickly realised that the car had been stolen from them. However, they were not likely to report the theft to the police.

Think

What would their reactions be when they read the *West Midlands Times* of Wednesday, January 3, and recognised the car?

Write

In the form of a script, write the conversation/argument which followed their reading of the newspaper report. (You might write dialogue which involves all three, or just two of them.)

West Midlands Times

Friday, January 5

JOYRIDE JEWELLERY

Further moves

ARTHUR PIRTON, 58, an antiques dealer from Rayton, Sussex, will be released from hospital today to travel to Brumsgrove. Police hope he will be able to identify items of jewellery recovered from the Horseshoe Corner joyride crash on Tuesday. Mr Pirton, who has been receiving treatment for injuries suffered in an armed robbery at his home, will be accompanied by two members of the West Sussex Serious Crimes Squad.

Incident report

The antiques dealer is the complainant, or victim of the crime. He has been asked to complete the form below. Imagine you are the antiques dealer. Copy the form and fill in the details.

WEST SUSSEX POLICE

Incident report: *Theft*

Name:

Address:

Date of birth:

Occupation:

Date of complaint:

Nature of complaint: *Armed robbery*

Items stolen:

Description/s of suspect/s:

Details of incident:

Signed:

Date:

The whole truth

A

B

C

D

E

F

G

H

The pictures tell part of the story.
Some of the 'boxes' have been left blank.

In order to complete the whole story, the illustrator needs more instructions.

What instructions would you give to the illustrator for each of the blank boxes so that s/he could tell your story accurately?

Now that you have all the ingredients, tell the whole story in the order in which the events happened.

You might wish to finish off the story by going beyond the point which is reached in these pages, and imagine what would become of some, or all, of the people involved.

A saucerful of worms

A saucerful of worms

Helen Fisher has been given the job of taking school harvest festival gifts to some old age pensioners. The last name on her list is 'Miss Brady. The Barge. The Canal.'

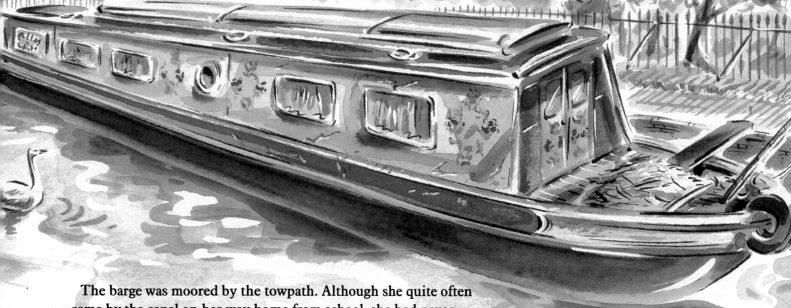

The barge was moored by the towpath. Although she quite often came by the canal on her way home from school, she had never seen it there before. Or perhaps it was just that she had not come by the canal for a long time. Frowning, she tried to remember.

The boat was long and low, and brightly painted. The hull was black, with green rubbing strakes and a red gunnel. The panels on the cabin sides were painted with roses – four flowers making a diamond shape. A striped green and red pole stuck out of the end. From a distance it looked like a picture in a book, but close to, Helen saw that some of the paint was peeling, and there was a heap of dirty straw on the small semi-circular poop-deck.

A plank led from the towpath to the deck, but Helen was not sure what to do. She could see the little cabin door with roses painted on it, but she was not sure she should go aboard. Crouching, she tried to see in through the windows, but the curtains were drawn.

Everything was quiet on the black water of the canal. The sun hung like a red balloon in the branches of the horse-chestnut tree. Only a swan came sailing, leaving a wake of ripples, from under the bridge. It was white on the water, all alone.

10

Questions

1 At what time of year does the story take place? How do you know?

2 If you were Helen, how would you feel as you approached the barge?

20 'Here, Cobbler! Here,
cob, cob, cob... Here, Cobbler!' called a voice from the barge.
'There's a good fellow. There's a grand lad.' It was an old voice.
The barge rocked gently as someone moved inside.

Helen stepped back. A thin yellow arm and hand appeared
through a window on the far side of the boat. The swan arched its
neck. A few scraps of bread floated towards him and he clicked at
them with his yellow beak. Wagging his white tail feathers, he
glided out of sight behind the barge.

The hand reappeared poking through the window, and tossed
30 some more bread. 'There's a grand old lad who can't sing for his
supper. There's my old faithful Cobbler,' said the voice.

Helen wished she had some bread to throw for the swan, but her
basket contained only the box of apples and oranges. Nothing that
swans liked, she thought. Anyway, at least she had a reason to go on
board.

She walked up the gang-plank. 'Hello?'

No one answered. Then the barge lurched. The cabin doors were
pushed open a crack.

'Who is it? What do you want?' The voice did not sound friendly.

40 'I'm Helen Fisher, from Heighton School. I've brought you a basket
from our harvest festival,' said Helen, for the seventh time today.

'Beg your pardon?' said the old voice. The cabin door opened a bit
wider, and an eye looked at her from the dark crack.

'I'm Helen Fisher. This is for you, from our harvest festival.'
She took the box of fruit from her basket.

The swan slid away nervously. Autumn leaves rippled against the
canal bank.

'Is it now? Then I expect you'll have to come in. Quickly, girl!'
The door was pushed open. Helen climbed
50 down the three steps of the companionway
and found herself standing before Miss Brady.

The old woman's hair was grey and white in
streaks, tied back in a bun. Her face was as thin
and brown as cardboard, with deep lines round
her nose and mouth. One leg was stretched stiffly
in a bandage, her heel resting on a coil of rope. She
was wearing a long brown skirt and a tweed jacket
with leather patches on the elbows. She still held a
slice of bread in her hand.

60 'Well, close the door.'
Helen pulled it shut with a bang.
'Shhh!' hissed Miss Brady. 'Now, talk quietly.'

Questions

3 What are your first
   impressions of Miss
   Brady, and why?

4 Think about what might
   happen next in the story.
   Do you think Helen will
   be made welcome by
   Miss Brady? What are
   your reasons?

Mrs Phillips had told Helen to speak up when she called on old age pensioners, but she did not dare disobey the fierce old woman.

'I'm Helen Fisher,' she whispered.

'Yes, yes, I heard,' snapped Miss Brady. 'Now what's this?'

Inside, the barge was long and thin and low, but surprisingly roomy. There were shelves, a small sink and cooker, bare boards, a black stove, and pieces of rope tied in incredible knots hanging on the cabin walls. A

70 cushion lay on the floor, with a hole torn in it and all its stuffing falling out.

'From our harvest festival,' Helen whispered. She looked at the old woman who was watching her suspiciously. There was a strange smell in the boat, strong and sour. On the floor were two saucers. One was full of milk and the other was full of... Helen looked again. It was full of raw liver and worms. Some of the worms wriggled.

'This is for me, is it? Well, well,' said the old woman. 'A booby prize for hurting my leg, I suppose.' She glanced at the box of fruit, but she did not seem pleased. 'Wonder which nosey do-gooder told them about me? Put it on the sink, out of harm's way.'

80 Surprised, Helen did as she was asked. All the other old people had been delighted or at least that's what they said. The sink and draining-board were quite small, like toys. Through a sliding door she could see a big heap of hay and leaves under a bunk. The cushion which made the seat of the bunk looked as if it had been slashed with a knife, and all the foam was bursting out. The smell was stronger, almost a stink.

.

At the end of this strange visit, Helen asks Miss Brady if there is anything she can do to help her. To her surprise Miss Brady asks her to get her a bucketful of worms and soil – even though she knows that Helen hates worms. Helen overcomes her dislike of worms and does as Miss Brady asks.

'Oh, it's you.' Miss Brady pushed open the cabin door. It was not much of a welcome.

'I've brought your worms, like I promised. Are you alright?' Miss

90 Brady's face was as yellow as sponge cake and there were black shadows under her cheekbones.

'Course I am!' snapped the old woman. 'Now keep your voice down, will you.'

'Sorry,' murmured Helen.

'It's Bad Bill,' said Miss Brady. 'Don't want to wake him. He's not in the best of tempers, bein' cooped up like this.'

'Who's Bad Bill?'

'Bad Bill the Badger.' Miss Brady pointed into the next cabin, where the dark lump of straw and hay was heaped under the bunk.

Questions

5 Having read this page, how have your ideas about Miss Brady changed and why?

6 We are about to meet a badger. How much do you know about badgers? Would you like to meet one close to?

100 Helen stared at the straw. 'A real badger, you mean?'

'Yes, yes. A real live kicking and biting badger.' She smiled at Helen. It made her face look better. 'And, thank the Lord, he's asleep.'

'A badger, on a barge?' Helen could not believe it. She had never seen a real badger. 'Is that what smells funny?'

'Same family as polecats, you know. They're all a bit smelly. Usually, he lives in a big pen down the canal, but I had to bring him with me when I hurt my ankle. Had to go to hospital, you see, for stitches. Couldn't just leave him. But it's no good, a badger on a boat, even if we are old friends.'

Miss Brady had a dry, posh voice. She clipped the ends off words and
110 addressed Helen as if she were a public meeting.

'Bad Bill,' said Helen. 'So badgers have names, even if swans don't.'

Miss Brady scowled at her, then she burst out laughing. 'Touché! You've nailed me there, Helen Fisher!'

Helen grinned. 'Shall I put the kettle on – seeing as I'm here.' She wanted to stay. She wanted to see the badger.

'Good idea,' said the old woman. 'Could do with a cuppa – the old devil had me up all night. Gallivantin' and rampagin' round the cabin. Tryin' to dig his way out, you know. Poor old Bill,' she added more gently. Her face went hard again. 'There's another mug in the
120 locker there – if you want to stay a mo.'

'Great!' said Helen. She poured tea for them both. 'Does he like worms, then? I can get you tons off me Dad's allotment if you want.'

'Worms, dead chicks, meat, maize, he's partial to all sorts. But his favourite is honey. He'd eat it until he was as fat as butter if I let him.'

Then, just as she seemed friendly, Miss Brady's voice changed.

'Quickly, girl! Get out of the door! Go on, hurry!'

She grabbed Helen by the arm, making her spill her tea, and thrust her towards the companion-way. She was surprisingly strong. Startled, Helen climbed out onto the deck. The door closed to a tiny crack behind
130 her.

She heard a rustle and a thud like a heavy ball bouncing.

'Sorry,' called Miss Brady. 'Didn't mean to frighten you – it's just that he's a bad-tempered old devil at the moment. Might just bite, you know.'

Helen breathed her relief. She'd thought Miss Brady had gone mad. 'Can I look?' she whispered.

'Yes. But keep still.'

Helen peered in through the crack. Beside her, the smell of damp earth rose from the bucket of worms
140 she had left on the deck. For the first time ever, she saw a badger.

Questions

7 Why is the badger on the barge?
8 Why does Miss Brady suddenly tell Helen to get out?
9 How would you have felt at this point, if you were Helen?

The black and grey striped head poked through the door, and then came the fat rippling skirting-board of his body. Like a grey shadow, he moved out of the far cabin – then he was like a fat bear, bouncing along, thumping the planks, making a chickering snuffling whinny, like a tiny horse. His claws clicked and scratched on the wood. He lifted his striped snout towards the old woman, as if he was looking at her from out of his black nose, then he buried his face in the milk, and slurped and guzzled, noisy as a pig.

150   'Heck. . .' whispered Helen. 'He's ace!'

'Come here, you silly old lump,' said Miss Brady. The badger came bouncing up to her, like a grey rug being shaken. He reared on his hind legs and she rubbed his small round ears. 'What are you doing up at this time of day?'

Helen half expected to hear him purr. He made a pleased snuffling noise and rushed back to his saucer of worms. Clock-clock, chop, went his teeth on the clicking saucer. When the worms were all gone he shoved his nose under the saucer and flipped it over. Sniffing here and there, he ambled back to the far cabin and nosed his way

160   back into the heap of straw. After a bit of shoving and snorting, he disappeared from view.

They were both silent a while longer. Then Miss Brady said, 'Coast's clear. You can come back in.'

'Would he really bite me?' He had looked very tame to Helen.

'Perhaps. Can't take chances. A wild badger wouldn't come near you, but that old devil might. Might think you're an unfriendly badger trespassing on his territory, you see.'

Helen nodded. 'I wish I had a badger for a pet.'

'Oh, he's no pet,' said Miss Brady, shaking her head. 'He's a trial and

170   a torment, bless him.' She gazed at the upturned saucer, the lines deepening around her thin nose and mouth. She continued talking, quietly, while the sight of the water made rippling reflections on the cabin wall above her head. 'I'm an obstinate old woman, Helen Fisher. Don't care for people – never have. Especially children. Can't bear brats.' She glanced up, her thin lips pressed tightly together.

Questions

10 How does Helen react to the badger? What does this tell us about her?

11 At the end of this page what further ideas have you got about Miss Brady?

Helen smiled. 'Don't you like me, even?' For a moment, she thought
the old woman was joking with her, but when she saw the look on Miss
Brady's face she knew she was not.

The old woman was not smiling at all. 'Probably not. Can't see why
180   I should change the habits of a life-time just for you, girl.'

Helen did not know what to say. Miss Brady baffled her. She wished
the badger would come out again. 'You must like somebody.'

'I must, must I? Hmmmph!' the old woman snorted.

'Well, I hate being lonely,' said Helen quietly.

'Do you?'

'Yes.'

'Me. I like it. Not lonely, but being alone. Suits me. Shall I tell
you something?'

Helen nodded.

190   'Hundreds of old people are lonely, and if you went to see them
they'd think the sun shone out of your eyes. Funny, isn't it? Here I
am, and the last thing I want is people. People fussing and changing
things.'

Helen felt she was being tested, or challenged. Miss Brady was
watching her across the cabin.

'I won't change anything,' she said.

'No,' said Miss Brady. 'No, I don't think you would.' She smiled
at Helen. 'Thank you for bringing the worms.'

Janni Howker: *Badger on the barge*

Portrait of Miss Brady

TF   These two extracts come from a story called 'Badger on the barge' by Janni Howker.
They give us a very vivid picture of Miss Brady, one of the main characters in the story.

1 What does she look like?
Go back through the story and find all the
places where the narrator tells us what Miss
Brady looks like. Write down the words that are
used and what they suggest to you.

2 How does she behave?
Look for descriptions of how she behaves: what
she does and how she moves. Make a note of
these. For each one, say what you think it tells
us about what she is like as a person.

3 What does she say?
Look at what she says and the way in which she
says it. Make a note of the important things she
says. Then note down what they tell us about
her character.

4 The whole picture
Look again at what you have written. Use it to
help you build up a whole picture of Miss Brady.
Write a description of her, using as much of the
evidence you have collected as possible.

Action and description

In 'Badger on the barge', Janni Howker has to describe a badger to people who have probably never seen one. We can learn a lot about writing by studying how she does this.

Comparisons

Similes

She compares the badger – which we may not have seen – to things that we probably have seen. She says it is *like* other things. We call these comparisons **similes**. All the similes in the extract on the right are marked in *italics*.

Metaphors

Sometimes a writer can use comparisons without telling the reader that s/he is doing so. Such comparisons are called **metaphors**. The metaphor in this extract is underlined.

The black and grey striped head poked through the door, and then came the <u>fat rippling skirting-board of his body</u>. *Like a grey shadow*, he moved out of the far cabin – then he was *like a fat bear*, bouncing along, thumping the planks, making a chickering snuffling whinny, *like a tiny horse*. His claws clicked and scratched on the wood. He lifted his striped snout towards the old woman, as if he was looking at her from out of his black nose, then he buried his face in the milk, and slurped and guzzled, *noisy as a pig*.

1   Janni Howker says that the badger is *like a grey shadow*. Remembering where the badger is when Helen first sees it, why do you think she makes this comparison?
2   Look at the picture of the badger on page 125. What aspects of the badger did Janni Howker have in mind when she wrote each of the other comparisons in this extract?
3   Look at the rest of the story and find other examples of similes and metaphors. Choose two that you like and explain why you find them striking or vivid.

What does it look like? How does it move?

Look at these photographs of an insect and a reptile. Choose one and say what it looks like and what it might remind you of when it moves.

Writing

Choose an animal that you know or have seen and write a description of how it moves and the noises it makes.

Gallivantin' and rampagin'

Sometimes writers want to put down on paper the exact way in which people speak. Janni Howker does this in her story 'Badger on the barge'. There are two things a writer can do.

Apostrophes

When we speak we often run words together and miss letters out. When we write this down, we need to show on paper that something is missing, so we use an apostrophe:

> I am   →   I'm
> gallivanting →   gallivantin'

Look through the story and find five other examples of this use of the apostrophe. For each one, write down the word(s) as they are printed and then the full version of the word(s).

Reminder

Apostrophes have another important use. They show that something belongs to someone or something.

- If the noun is **singular** and **does not end in s**, add 's

  my father's house

- If the noun is **plural** (more than one) and **ends in s**, add '

  my two friends' father

Writing sounds

When people are talking, they sometimes make sounds that are not real words:

'You must like somebody.'
'I must, must I? Hmmmph!' the old woman snorted.

What sort of sound do you think Miss Brady made? Try saying it aloud. Now think about the kind of noise people make in the following situations. For each one write it down as accurately as you can.

1 When they are unsure and trying to make up their mind about the answer to a question.
2 When they are very cold.
3 When they unexpectedly touch something very hot.
4 When they tread on something unpleasant.
5 When they are in a dark, spooky place and are frightened.
6 When they eat something they really like.

Canal boat holiday

This page and the following four pages take the form of a scrapbook made by a family who went on a canal boat holiday. It contains photographs, extracts from a diary, a map and other information that they collected as they went. Read it through and then look at the activities on page 134.

A modern canal boat

This cutaway diagram illustrates a modern narrow boat built for pleasure cruising. It shows:

1 toilet
2 single bed
3 double bed
4 lounge area with
   – sitting area
   – dining area
5 bath/shower
6 kitchen
7 storage for clothing.

West Midlands Canals

Map labels:
Shropshire Union Canal, PENKRIDGE, Autherley Junction, BREWOOD, Aldersley Junction, Staffs & Worcs Canal, Birmingham Canal Navigators, Fradley Junction, BURTON ON TRENT, Trent & Mersey Canal, SHARDLOW, Trent Junction, LOUGHBOROUGH, River Soar, SNARESTONE, LEICESTER, EAST MIDLANDS RING, Fazeley Junction, Ashby Canal, Coventry Canal, No Through Routes, STOURPORT, Birmingham and Fazeley Canal Navigators, BIRMINGHAM, MIDLANDS RING, Hawkesbury Junction, Leicester Canal, WELFORD, River Severn, STOURPORT RING, North Stratford Canal, Grand Union Canal, COVENTRY, North Oxford Canal, Worcs & B'ham Canal, Kings Norton, RUGBY, WORCESTER, STOKE PRIOR, Kingswood Junction, WARWICK, LEAMINGTON SPA, South Stratford Canal, NAPTON, Braunston Junction, Norton Junction, Gayton Junction, NORTHAMPTON, AVON RING, STRATFORD UPON AVON, BANBURY, STOKE BRUERNE, River Avon, EVESHAM, South Oxford Canal, TEWKESBURY, GLOUCESTER

1 Stourport-on-Severn

Stourport is where the Staffordshire & Worcestershire Canal joins the River Severn (the longest river in Britain). There's a big 'basin' where boats tie up and you can get food and other supplies. It's quite a famous waterways centre.

You can go up the Staffordshire & Worcestershire Canal to Great Haywood (where it joins the Trent and Mersey Canal), or you can go down the Severn to Worcester.

2 Worcester

A cathedral city on the River Severn. It is where the Worcester & Birmingham Canal starts – at Diglis Basin. Like Stourport, this is a popular place for canal boats to start and finish their journeys, and take on fuel and provisions. It's near the Royal Worcester Porcelain Factory.

3 The Stratford-upon-Avon Canal

A canal through Shakespeare Country! It starts at Kings Norton – just outside Birmingham and goes all the way to Stratford-upon-Avon.

On the way you see lovely old cottages with funny barrel-roofs. Also there are often little split bridges over the canal.

4 Stratford-upon-Avon

In Stratford the canal goes right into the middle of the town. You can tie up just in front of the Royal Shakespeare Theatre. We spent some time wandering round the town and went to visit Shakespeare's Birthplace (it's in Henley Street and has a great many exhibits connected with Shakespeare). We also went to another place called the Shakespeare Experience – which was fun.

If you come to Stratford along the canal, you can go through a lock into the River Avon and travel all the way down to Tewkesbury, where the Avon joins the River Severn.

5 Worcester & Birmingham Canal – going through a lock

When a canal goes uphill, you have to use locks. In some places the slope is quite steep, so you have several locks very close to each other. We went up through the Tardebigge locks – there are thirty of them in about two miles! (You can do them in three hours, but we took half a day.)

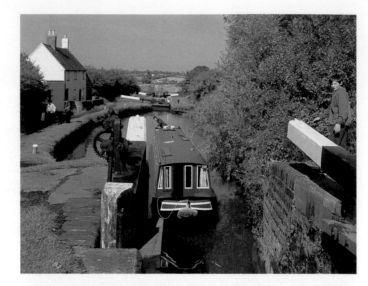

6

If the water in the lock is at the wrong level you have to raise or lower it by raising the paddle – this lets water pass from the higher level to the lower level.

When the level of the water in the lock is the same as the level of the boat, you can open the lock gate and let the boat in.

7

Then you have to get the water in the lock to the same level as the water in the canal – so if you are 'locking up', you have to raise it. With both sets of lock gates closed, you open the top paddle. When the water in the lock is at the same level as the water in the canal (in the direction you are going in) then you can open the lock gates.

How a lock works

Typical narrow lock

At a lock the canal narrows. The water level is higher at the top end than it is at the bottom. The lock itself is enclosed by single or double gates which can be opened by pushing on a balance beam. There are openings which will allow water to pass from the higher level into the lock and from the lock into the lower level. The openings are covered by movable paddles. The paddles are wound up to allow the water to pass through.

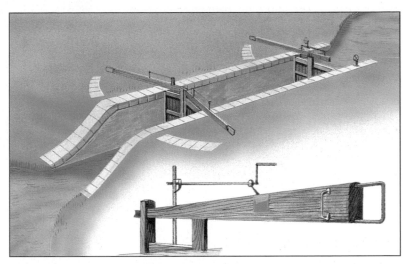

Locking up

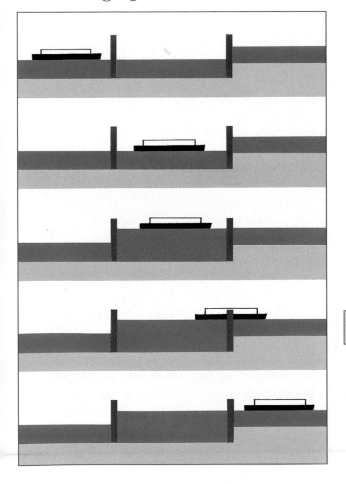

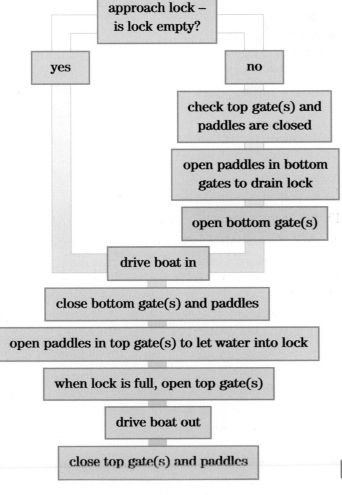

approach lock – is lock empty?

yes

no

check top gate(s) and paddles are closed

open paddles in bottom gates to drain lock

open bottom gate(s)

drive boat in

close bottom gate(s) and paddles

open paddles in top gate(s) to let water into lock

when lock is full, open top gate(s)

drive boat out

close top gate(s) and paddles

Writing

All the writing activities on this page are based on the words and pictures on pages 129–133. There are detailed instructions for each activity, but before you start any of them, read this advice:

- think carefully about the information you need before you start writing
- look at pages 129–133 and find the information you need
- decide whether you need extra information – if so, you may need to go to the library
- make notes, using your own words as far as possible
- use your notes as you write your first draft.

1 Information book

You have been asked to write a page in an information book for readers aged 7–9. This is your 'brief' (instructions):

Main topic: canals

what a canal is – history – uses today

Sub-topic: locks

what they are for – how they work

Advice

Use pictures as much as possible.

KEEP IT SIMPLE!

You can choose pictures from pages 129–133, or draw the pictures yourself, or you can write a detailed 'artwork brief'. An artwork brief is a set of instructions to an artist, explaining in detail what you want the artist to draw.

2 Instruction manual

Some friends are going on a canal boat holiday for the first time. They are not too sure about how to go through a lock. Write a set of instructions explaining how to 'lock down'. (See page 135 for advice on giving instructions.)

3 Advertisement

You are working for a company, based in Stratford-upon-Avon, that hires out canal boats. You have been asked to design an advertisement in full colour for the company's weekly holidays, to take up a whole page in a family travel and holiday magazine. The idea is that people will be so attracted by your advertisement that they will write or telephone for your company's holiday brochure.

You should decide what your main 'selling points' are. They might be some or all of these points:

- the boats are modern and comfortable
- it is an active holiday
- the canals and waterways pass through beautiful countryside
- you can 'get away from it all'
- you can visit some interesting towns
- it is a holiday that is definitely 'different'.

Write the text for the advertisement, and decide what illustration(s) you want to use. You can choose from those on pages 129–133, or you can decide to use different ones. If so, you must describe exactly what you want.

Giving instructions

Think of your audience

Ask yourself:
- Do I understand the process properly myself?
- Which parts of it are the tricky ones to understand?
- How much does my audience know already?
- Are there any technical terms that I need to explain?
- Are there any points at which they are likely to get lost?
- Would it help if I used diagrams?

Then use a drafting approach:
1. Think through the questions you asked yourself.
2. Make a written plan: list the main points in order.
3. Check the list is completed in the right order.
4. Write your first draft.
5. Get someone else to read it and comment on it.
6. Draft it again … until it's crystal clear.

Grammar

Instructions often take this form:

Take the grommet in your left hand.
Turn it to the right.

Sentences like this are called **directives**. They are different from statement sentences in one important way:

	subject	**verb**	**rest of sentence**
statement	*She*	*turns*	*it to the right.*
directive		*Turn*	*it to the right.*

Directives are sometimes called commands. In fact we use directives for several different purposes, not just to give instructions.

> **Remember**
> There are four types of sentence:
>
> **Statement**
> She is driving the car.
>
> **Question**
> Whose car is she driving?
>
> **Directive**
> Stop the car.
>
> **Exclamation**
> What a terrible driver you are!

What's what?

1. Match the sentence and the purpose.

PURPOSE	SENTENCE
1 to command	A *Have a good journey!*
2 to request	B *Try a different colour.*
3 to warn	C *Get out of my house!*
4 to invite	D *Come to the pictures with me.*
5 to advise	E *Watch out!*
6 to wish well	F *Give me a hand, please.*

2. Make up one sentence of your own for each of the purposes in the table.

You can't take it with you

Page	Title	What you do	Why you do it
137	**You can't take it with you**	Look at some pictures and think about money, and valuable possessions.	To start you thinking about the themes of the unit.
138–142	**Forty for a penny**	Read a story and answer questions about it. Study accent and dialect. Talk about sweets. Write about a midnight feast.	To develop your reading and writing skills. To learn about accent and dialect.
143	**Punctuation**	Learn about colons and semi-colons.	To develop your knowledge of punctuation.
144–147	**It's a bargain... or is it?**	Study text and pictures about customers' rights and answer questions about what you have just learnt. Act out a role play with a partner.	To develop your close reading skills. To develop your ability to solve problems. To learn how to role play.
148	**Money – what people think**	Find out what people really think about money. Think about the best way of getting the information you need. Report your findings to the group.	To learn how to find out information from other people and how to present your findings.
149	**Asking the right question**	Learn about how to ask good questions in an interview.	To develop your interviewing skills. To learn more about how sentences work.
150–151	**The miser**	Read two passages and answer questions about them. Relate the passages to the present day.	To make you think about how things have changed since the passages were written. To develop your skills as a writer.
152	**Wordbuilding Wordpower**	Learn about how words are put together to make different meanings. Look again at some of the words used in the unit.	To develop your vocabulary and spelling.

You can't take it with you

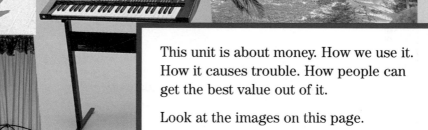

This unit is about money. How we use it. How it causes trouble. How people can get the best value out of it.

Look at the images on this page.

- Which pictures appeal to you? Why?
- Which pictures have no appeal? Why?
- What would you want to add to this collection of what money can buy?
- What is your most valued possession?
- What is the thing you would most like to own?

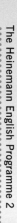

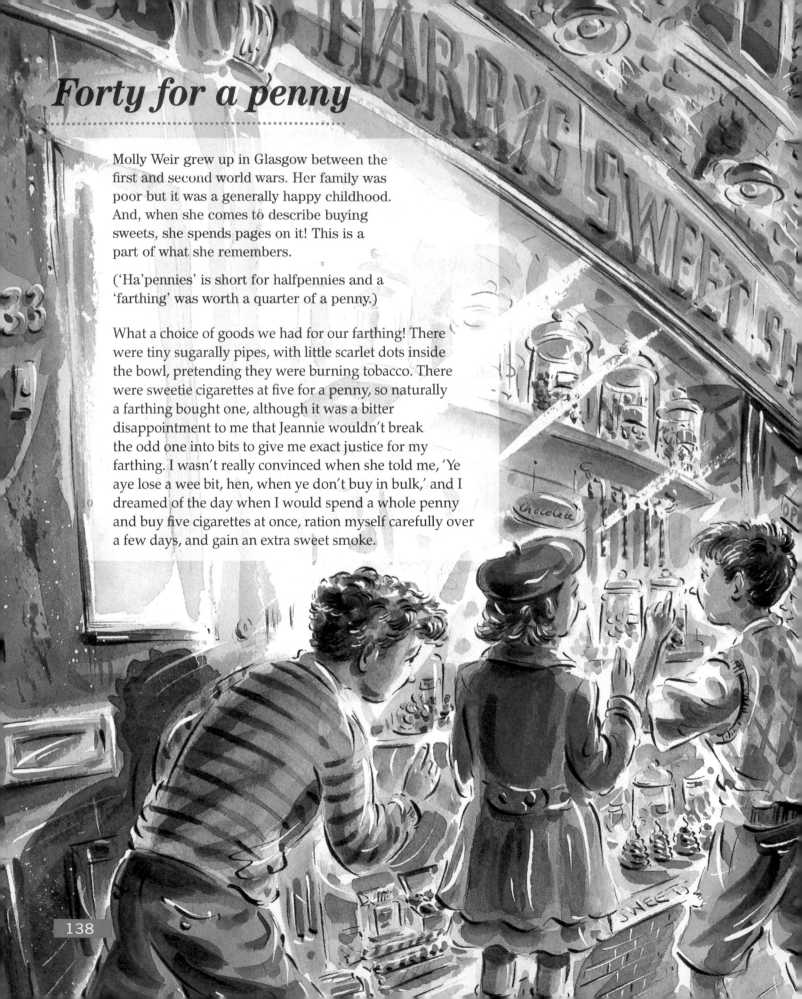

Forty for a penny

Molly Weir grew up in Glasgow between the first and second world wars. Her family was poor but it was a generally happy childhood. And, when she comes to describe buying sweets, she spends pages on it! This is a part of what she remembers.

('Ha'pennies' is short for halfpennies and a 'farthing' was worth a quarter of a penny.)

What a choice of goods we had for our farthing! There were tiny sugarally pipes, with little scarlet dots inside the bowl, pretending they were burning tobacco. There were sweetie cigarettes at five for a penny, so naturally a farthing bought one, although it was a bitter disappointment to me that Jeannie wouldn't break the odd one into bits to give me exact justice for my farthing. I wasn't really convinced when she told me, 'Ye aye lose a wee bit, hen, when ye don't buy in bulk,' and I dreamed of the day when I would spend a whole penny and buy five cigarettes at once, ration myself carefully over a few days, and gain an extra sweet smoke.

Sweeties had been very expensive after war No I and tumbling prices came along in the nick of time for me to enjoy them. Never will I forget the day when the number of aniseed balls went up to forty a penny. There were queues at the wee shop that day, and it was indeed a land of plenty to be given ten balls, hard as iron, for a farthing. I nearly sucked my tongue raw until, with dawning disbelief, I realised I'd have to leave some over for next day. For sweeties to last more than a few minutes was outside my experience until that moment, and it was a marvellous feeling to tuck that wee poke with the three remaining aniseed balls behind Grannie's hankies in the bottom of the chest of drawers, where my brothers couldn't make a raid without either Grannie or me spotting them.

My purchases were always made with farthings and ha'pennies, with maybe a penny when I was going to the Saturday matinee, but beyond those sums I never ventured to think. I never thought of my precious 'savings' as spending money. I put them away and they were as safe as if they were in the Bank of England. But one dizzy day when we were playing 'guesses' in front of Mrs Frame's window a drunk neighbour came up and surveyed us solemnly, blinking as he swayed, listening to our excited 'guesses' and stumbling in exasperation as we rushed past him across to the edge of the pavement when we had made our guess. The edge of the pavement was the finishing line for the winner. When we played guesses with shop goods like this we gave the initial letters of an article in the window, say JB for jelly babies, or WCB for whipped cream bon-bons, and the first to yell out the correct answer leaped for the pavement edge to win. A flight of fancy now made me give PARTW as mine, and when nobody guessed it, my triumphant yells of 'Putty all round the windows' brought a glimmer to the drunk man's face.

He fumbled in his pocket and brought out a handful of coppers. We stood silent, watching him. We were forbidden to talk to strangers, and certainly to drunk men, but we knew this one, alas, for he was a fairly new neighbour. 'Here's a ha'penny for each o' you,' he said ponderously. 'And you, the wee lassie that made the putty guess, here's tuppence for you.' Tuppence! For nothing! It was a miracle. It was a fortune.

As I looked at the two coppers, a daring thought sent my head spinning and twisted my stomach with excitement. This money had come for nothing. I hadn't earned it, so I needn't spend it carefully. It was riches galore. I determined to enjoy the thrill of real spending. I drew a deep breath. 'Can I spend it a' on one thing, mister?' I asked. 'On whit?' he said, puzzled. 'On one thing,' I repeated patiently. 'Instead of a faurden's woth of this and a ha'penny worth o' that?'

'Spend it on wey ye like,' he replied grandly as he turned unsteadily towards his house. 'Enjoy yersel', hen, ha'e a real burst.'

I turned to the window and examined every single thing slowly and deliberately. It must be something really wickedly extravagant. Something which wouldn't last, a luxury that would have to be eaten all at once if its flavour and filling were to be fully enjoyed. Suddenly I saw what I wanted.

The others had spent their ha'pennies by the time I went inside the shop, and were chewing happily, waiting for me. There was an awed silence as I demanded imperiously, 'A whipped cream walnut, please.' Mrs Frame smiled and turned to the box. A burst of excited whispering broke out from my chums. 'She's spendin' her hale tuppence on one thing.' 'Fancy buying a walnut, and it's that wee.' 'Don't buy it Molly,' urged one chum. 'It'll a' burst when you bite it, an' ye'll no' be able to keep any till the morn.'

I smiled, deaf to reason, and my teeth fell exultantly on my whole tuppence-worth. It was a glorious moment. I enjoyed every extravagant bite, and I included that drunk man in my prayers for quite a while afterwards.

Molly Weir: *Forty for a penny*

Questions A

All these questions are about lines 1–26.

1 How much pocket money did the children regularly receive?
2 What had made sweets expensive?
3 What caused queues at the sweet shop?
4 How many aniseed balls did Molly eat that day?
5 What did she do with the ones she had left?
6 Why were they safe then?

Questions B

These questions are about the whole passage.

7 Why was Molly disappointed that she only received one sweet cigarette for a farthing?
8 Why did she nearly suck her tongue raw?
9 What did she find so amazing about the aniseed balls?
10 How did the children know that the neighbour they met was drunk?
11 Why did he give Molly twopence?
12 What 'daring thought' sent her head 'spinning'?
13 What did the others think of her extravagance?

Questions C

These questions are about the whole passage.
Answer them as fully as you can.

14 What does Jeannie mean when she says, 'Ye aye lose a wee bit, hen, when ye don't buy in bulk'?
15 On what occasions did Molly spend more than a halfpenny on sweets, and why do you think this was?
16 What were the rules of the guessing game the children played?
17 What does Molly mean when she describes herself as 'deaf to reason'?
18 What are the most important ways in which the life Molly Weir describes is:

- similar to yours
- different from yours?

Accent and dialect

This story is set in Glasgow and the people in it speak with a Glaswegian **accent**. Molly Weir shows how they pronounce their words by the way in which she spells them. They also use the local **dialect** and the story contains a number of words and expressions that do not occur in Standard English. Go through the text and make a table like the one below.

Accent		Dialect	
Her spelling	Normal spelling	Word/Expression	Standard English
Whit	What	wee	little

Discussing sweets

1 What are your favourite sweets? What do you like about them?
2 Are there any sweets you can't stand? Why?
3 What sweets can you think of that you can no longer buy?
4 If you had £2 and had been told to buy a variety of sweets for you and your friends, what would you choose?
5 Think about the kinds of sweet (or sweet food) that you like a lot but don't get very often. What would be your best sweet treat of all?

The midnight feast

Write a story about a midnight feast. When you are planning it, think about these things:

- Where does the feast take place?
- Who is to be there at the feast?
- What sweets/other food will there be?
- What happens at the feast itself?
- Do any adults discover you?
- How do they react if they do?

Note
If your writing contains any lists, you may need to use colons. Look on page 143 for advice about this.

You can't take it with you

142

Punctuation

Introducing the colon...

Colons are used:

■ to introduce a list:

The key things to remember are:
- *go back to the shop as soon as possible*
- *take your receipt or some other proof of purchase.*

■ before a piece of speech, instead of a comma:

He stood up and spoke to the whole class: 'Unless I find out who did this, I shall have to punish you all.'

...and the semi-colon

This is a very useful punctuation mark. It is stronger than a comma, but not as strong as a full stop:

✔ *It was a great bargain; I've not seen it cheaper anywhere else and I don't think I ever will.*

you can't just put a comma:

✘ *It was a great bargain, I've not seen it cheaper anywhere else and I don't think I ever will.*

and a full stop would break up two ideas which ought to stay together:

✘ *It was a great bargain. I've not seen it cheaper anywhere else and I don't think I ever will.*

Practice

Copy out this passage, putting in all the necessary punctuation marks. Do not turn back to check!

and now lennie you have won over three thousand dollars in cash and merchandise and more important you have won the chance to spin our vacation wheel how do you feel about that lennie real good sir then join me over here at the vacation wheel now lennie i dont have to remind you that up there on the wheel are twenty all-expense paid vacations to places all over the world do i no sir thats twenty all-expense paid vacations you can go to rome to london to paris you can go to beautiful hawaii exotic mexico or sunny spain all in all there arc twenty wonderful all-expense paid vacations up there on the wheel but lennie as you know there are also what we call our zonk trips how do you feel about those lennie well i hope i dont get one and thats what were hoping too arent we folks hear that applause lennie theyre all with you now step up close to the vacation wheel thats right the three zonk trips as we call them are here and here and here try not to land on them i will sir all right put up your hand now lennie right here on the vacation wheel and lennie give it a spin here goes

It's a bargain...or is it?

TF

You've got some Christmas cash burning a hole in your pocket, the sales are on and you're ready to spend, spend, spend. But beware! Those tempting bargains may not be as good as they seem. Check out our guide to sales speak to make sure your bargain is one to brag about.

What if your bargain's a disaster?

10 Anything you buy, whether it's in a sale or not, has to live up to three rules known as the Sale of Goods Act. This handy law says that what you buy has to work properly, do the job it's meant to, and match up to the way it's described on the packaging or advert.

If it doesn't do these things you can ask for your money back. Shops may offer you a repair, a replacement, or a credit note, but you don't have to accept these if you don't want to. If you can, try your bargain out before parting 20 with your cash, or at least check it over as soon as you get home. If you've got a duff buy, take it back straightaway – if you hang on to it too long you may lose your right to a refund (though they should still exchange or repair it). A shopkeeper doesn't have to help if you simply change your mind: it's up to you to pick the right thing first off. So if you decide that jacket doesn't suit you after all, the shop doesn't have to exchange it – although they 30 might do out of goodwill.

No refunds on sale goods
Shops aren't allowed to say this. If you buy something which turns out to be faulty you're entitled to your money back – whether you bought it in a sale or not.

Special purchase – buy while stocks last!
There shouldn't be anything wrong with these – but it may mean they've over-ordered, or it was a job lot going cheap. Your lucky day, or that they can't sell for higher prices?

Cut price
Cut price from what? The tag should show you what the original price was.

Seconds
There might be a fault in the material or the stitching, for example. Check what the fault is and decide if you mind while you're still in the shop – you won't be able to use the fault as a reason for taking the jeans back later.

Display model
This may be a bit scratched or dirty – ask the shop assistant what condition it's in. But unless they say otherwise, the game should still work perfectly – if it doesn't, you should get a refund.

'I'd like my money back, please'

Taking something back to the shop may sound about as much fun as having your headteacher round to tea, but if you act cool and stick to your guns you'll be OK. The key things to remember are:

✪ go back to the shop as soon as possible

✪ take your receipt, or some other proof of purchase

✪ explain the problem and ask for your money back

✪ be calm and polite
(more effective than getting upset)

✪ ask to speak to the manager if the assistant won't help

✪ be persistent – don't let them fob you off!

40

A tale of two watches...

Rosemin Manji, 16, from West Sussex
'In the sales last December I bought a watch for £1 from a bargain shop that claimed to have a "closing down" sale. I brought the item home and it worked for about five minutes! I didn't bother to return it since I was given no receipt and I thought it my own fault for buying something so cheap and expecting it to last. The "closing down" sale is still going on.'

Nelson Reynolds, 12, from County Londonderry
'I was looking for a new watch, I had £10 that Grandad had sent for my birthday and if necessary I was going to add some pocket money to it. I saw a "Citizen" watch which I liked, but there was no price on it. I enquired about the price and was told that the box and instructions were missing so it was reduced from £64.99 to £12.99. The watch came with a four year guarantee that included the battery and we had three weeks of fun finding out what all the buttons were for. It was a great bargain; I've not seen it cheaper anywhere else and I don't think I ever will.'

Only £8.99 (ex. VAT)
Beware 'bargain' prices like this which say they don't include VAT (value added tax) – this will add on an extra 17.5%. Get those calculators out!

Shop-soiled
You'll need to give these a wash, but they should be OK otherwise – check with the assistant. If you later find they are damaged you should get a refund.

Huge discounts in all departments!
But do they include anything you actually want to buy?

Best price ever!
Best according to whom? It may be the best for that shop, but could still be cheaper down the road.

Buy two and get one free!
But do you want even one of them, let alone three? And how much extra are they asking for the two you buy?

Young shoppers' problems

Can you answer these young shoppers' questions?
Your answers must be based on the information on pages 144–145.

1 Emma bought a skirt in a sale that was marked 'seconds'. She looked at it carefully and found that one of the seams needed sewing up. Emma reckoned she could manage that but when she got home and tried the skirt on again, the split became much worse and Emma decided that it was beyond her sewing skills. When she took it back, the shop refused to exchange it. Emma wants to know if this is legal, and why?

2 Waz bought a pair of jeans in a sale and they were marked as shop-soiled. He washed them when he got home and the marks on one leg did not come off. He washed them again in one of those biological, stain-digesting powders. Still the marks did not come off. When Waz took the jeans back to the shop, they refused to exchange them on the basis that they had been clearly marked as 'shop-soiled'. Are they right? Waz wants to know.

3 Carolyn bought a jacket which she and her friend really liked. It was expensive because it was not in the sale. When they got home, Carolyn thought the colour looked quite different to how it had looked in the shop. In fact, she didn't like it. Her friend agreed and they took it back. The people in the shop were very polite but refused to take it back because there was nothing wrong with it. Carolyn wants to find out if the shop is allowed to do that.

4 The new hand-held computer game that Ranjit bought in town worked perfectly...for the first seven minutes of the bus ride home. Then it conked out. Nothing! Not a bleep! The next day he took it back to the shop who did not have another one. They offered to have it repaired or to give him a credit note. He would prefer to have his money back in order to buy it somewhere else. Can he insist?

Role play

Work with a partner.
Choose one of these two situations.

A

Prepare a scene where one of you is politely trying to convince a manager to take back an item which is not faulty but which you have decided you don't want.

Decide first on the item you are taking back.

B

Prepare a scene in which you politely try to get a refund on something that you believe to be faulty.

Top tips

Prepare a top ten tips for shopping in the sales based on what you have discovered from this section. The tips should be aimed at young teenagers.

Solving the problem

Write a letter to the headquarters of a chain of shops, taking up the case of Emma, Waz, Carolyn or Ranjit and trying to find a solution.

Money – what people think

The challenge

- Find out what people think and feel about money.
- Make a spoken report (of one or two minutes) on what you find out.

What to do

1 Decide…
what aspect of the subject to research. For example:

- What would people do if they won a million pounds?
- What is the minimum wage a person needs to live on?
- How much money do you need to feed a family of four for a week?
- How has the way people spend money changed in the last twenty years?
- What is the worst thing about having money?
- What is the worst thing about being short of money?

2 List…
the questions you want to ask. You need a **main question**, which could be one of the questions listed above. You also need some **follow-up questions**. These will help you find out in more detail what people think. **There is further information and advice about questions on the facing page**.

3 Plan…
who you will question (and when and where).

4 Ask…
your questions.

5 Note…
the answers you receive.

6 Prepare…
your report to the group. Organise your ideas. (You may want to write some notes, but don't write it all down. If you do, it just sounds boring.) You could even practise it on your own.

7 Report…
your findings to the group.

Asking the right question

We asked Jenni Mills, a well-known radio journalist, what kinds of questions an interviewer should ask. This is what she told us.

TF

The main problem that a lot of people have when they are interviewing, is that they start off with a question like, 'Do you find that it is difficult writing novels?' for example. The answer to that is, 'No'. You have to draw your interviewee out to say a bit more than that.

The best way is to rephrase the question. If you say, 'How difficult do you find it writing novels?' immediately the person you are interviewing has got to say more than 'No'. They have got to put their answer into a proper sentence; they've got to say, 'Well actually I find it remarkably easy writing novels.' Once they've got that first sentence out, it is amazing how other sentences will flow from it. So it is always best to start your question with a <u>who</u>, <u>what</u>, <u>why</u>, <u>how</u>, kind of word.

The other thing that I find is really helpful when I'm doing interviews, is to ask people to describe things to me: I say to them, 'Describe what it's like doing this, that or the other', 'Describe how you felt when this happened.' There are all sorts of little tricks like that that you can use, that will get more than that kind of bored 'Yes' or 'No' or 'Not really'.

But if you ask these 'Did you', 'Have you' questions you'll almost inevitably end up getting yeses and noes.

Different kinds of question

Jenni Mills mentions two kinds of question:

Question type	Answer expected
Yes/No question	*Yes, No, I don't know*
Wh- question (open)	*Some kind of more detailed information*

There is one other kind of question, although it is less common than the other two:

Do you prefer apples or pears?

This is called an **alternative** question.

As Jenni Mills points out, the best kind of question for the interviewer is a Wh- question, because it is open: it does not limit what the person can reply. Yes/No and alternative questions don't allow the other person much choice of answer.

Wh- questions

Who?
What?
Which?
When?
Where?
Why?
How?

The miser

At night he closed his shutters, and made fast his doors, and drew forth his gold. Long ago the heap of coins had become too large for the iron pot to hold them, and he had made for them two thick leather bags, which wasted no room in their resting place, but lent themselves flexibly to every corner. How the guineas shone as they came pouring out of dark leather mouths! The silver bore no large proportion in amount to the gold, because the long pieces of linen which formed his chief work were always partly paid for in gold, and out of the silver he supplied his own bodily wants, choosing always the shillings and sixpences to spend in this way. He loved the guineas best, but he would not change the silver – the crowns and half-crowns that were his own earnings, begotten by his labour; he loved them all. He spread them out in heaps and bathed his hands in them; then he counted them and set them up in regular piles, and felt their rounded outline between his thumb and fingers, and thought fondly of the guineas that were only half-earned by the work in his loom, as if they had been unborn children – thought of the guineas that were coming slowly through the coming years, through all his life, which spread far away before him, the end quite hidden by countless days of weaving. No wonder his thoughts were still with his loom and his money when he made his journeys through the fields and the lanes to fetch and carry home his work, so that his steps never wandered to the hedge-banks and the lane-side in search of the once familiar herbs; these too belonged to the past, from which his life had shrunk away, like a rivulet that has sunk far down from the grassy fringe of its old breadth into a little shivering thread, that cuts a groove for itself in the barren sand.

But about the Christmas of that fifteenth year, a second great change came over Marner's life.

George Eliot: *Silas Marner*

Thinking about the passage

1. Look at what Silas Marner does before he gets out his money. What does that tell you about him?
2. How does George Eliot get across the sense of just how much money there is?
3. Select the phrases that give you a sense of how Silas Marner loves money. Say why you chose them.
4. What do we learn about Silas Marner's life apart from his love of money?
5. What do you think of Silas Marner?
6. What might happen to change Silas Marner's life?
7. Now compare the description of Silas Marner with another famous account of a miser, from Charles Dickens' *A Christmas Carol*:

> Oh! but he was a tight-fisted hand at the grindstone, Scrooge! a squeezing, wrenching, clutching, covetous old sinner! Hard and sharp as flint, from which no steel had ever struck out generous fire; secret, and self-contained, and solitary as an oyster. The cold within him froze his old features, nipped his pointed nose, shrivelled his cheek, stiffened his gait; made his eyes red, his thin lips blue; and spoke out shrewdly in his grating voice. A frosty rime was on his head, and on his eyebrows, and his wiry chin. He carried his own low temperature always about with him; he iced his office in the dog-days; and didn't thaw it one degree at Christmas.

10

Compare the ways in which George Eliot and Charles Dickens describe their subjects. What would you say were the similarities and the differences?

Writing

Imagine a modern miser. What kind of person would you think of as a miser today? Think about:

- what they would hoard
- how and where they would keep it
- how they would feel about it
- how they would behave towards other people
- what they would look like.

Now write your description of *A modern miser*.

Wordbuilding

Many words are made from smaller words joined together. When Molly Weir finds she has been given twopence she decides to spend it on 'something that wouldn't last'. *Something* is one of those words made from two smaller words: *some* and *thing*. How many words can you make out of this group of words:

play	your	every
under	set	up
day	less	time
self	take	ground
price	some	no
where	land	over
dream	thing	help

Wordpower

All these words are in the unit you have been reading.

1 Explain the meaning of as many as you can.
2 For those you cannot explain, find them in the unit and try to work out their meaning from the sentence they are in.
3 For any that are left, look them up in a dictionary.
4 Make sure you can spell them all.

word	page	line	word	page	line	word	page	line
disbelief	139	20	solemnly	139	35	begotten	150	19
precious	139	30	exasperation	139	36	rivulet	150	44
fumbled	140	50	awed	140	78	grindstone	151	1
forbidden	140	52	seconds	144	–	covetous	151	2
goodwill	144	30	receipt	145	38	gait	151	7

Whose body is it?

Mr Robert Carson, the caretaker of your school, Pershott High, goes to open it up at 6.00 am on Monday 19th October for the cleaning staff. He finds the building as he left it except for one thing...

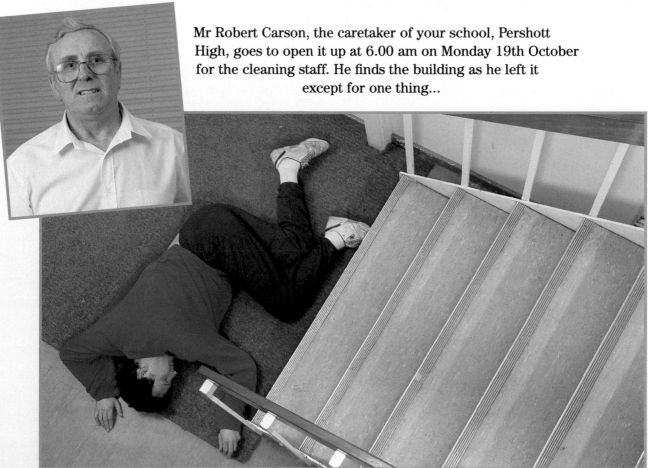

What do you think?

- What do you think has happened here?
- Who is the mystery person?
- How did he come to be at the bottom of the stairs?
- Is he dead or alive?

Decisions, decisions

1 What actions does Mr Carson, the caretaker, need to take?
2 In what order should he take them?
3 Think of as many explanations of this situation as you can.
4 Place them in order with the most likely explanation first.

Do not turn over until you have finished this!

The Heinemann English Programme 2

Still breathing

Mr Carson telephones for the emergency services and they arrive just before quarter past six. The police are on the scene about a minute before the ambulance service. The paramedics in the ambulance confirm that the man is still alive but appears to be in a coma.

He is taken to Pershott General Hospital where he is placed in intensive care. The registrar who was responsible for the admission, Dr Nadia Sahir, provides the police with this information about the patient.

Pershott General Hospital

19th October

Person found at Pershott High School

male

5 foot 11 inches

medium build

approximately 25–30 years old

brown hair

blue eyes

6-inch scar on upper right arm

no other distinguishing features

bruising to back of head – it is not possible to say whether this is the result of a blow received or a fall

The hospital staff also pass over to the police the following items that the man was carrying. None of the items carries a name.

The police report

Imagine you are the police officer who is responsible for this case. You need to make a record of:

■ what happened
■ what you found
■ possible explanations of what has happened
■ what you need to investigate now.

Later the same day

Towards the end of the day at Pershott High School, Rachel Karim and the rest of 8NW are waiting in the corridor to be dismissed by Miss Johnson after their swimming lesson in the school pool. Rachel notices a white plastic bag in the corner under the stairs at the end of the corridor. She asks her teacher if she can check if it is the bag she lost about a week ago with some of her books in it. It proves to be a disappointment for Rachel: it belongs to someone else. The bag is handed into the school office. The contents of the bag are pictured here.

Johnno

One man
who can chan
Who is he?
Can he be found befo...

THE DAY OF
THE
JACKAL
FREDERICK FORSYTH

Optima Sports Centre

Member

JOHN DAVIES

Optima Sports Centre

Member

STEVEN MARKS

Richard Storge
Dental Surgeon
141 Pershott Road
Pershott
PD1 8MR

Your next appointment is:
29 September at 2:30 pm
21 October at 4:00 pm
at /
at /

SALMON
Cameracolour
Post Card

Dear Waxy,
Bournemouth is
lousy. Marky
snores like a wild
animal. Wish I
was at home
watching paint dry.
Cheers Johnno

Mr M James
17 Fermeston Street
Pershott
PD7 4DH

When the school office staff check the bag, they are unable to link it up with any of the pupils. The school secretary telephones the police who take the bag away for investigation.

The police have had no further leads during the day so the bag is their first real breakthrough.

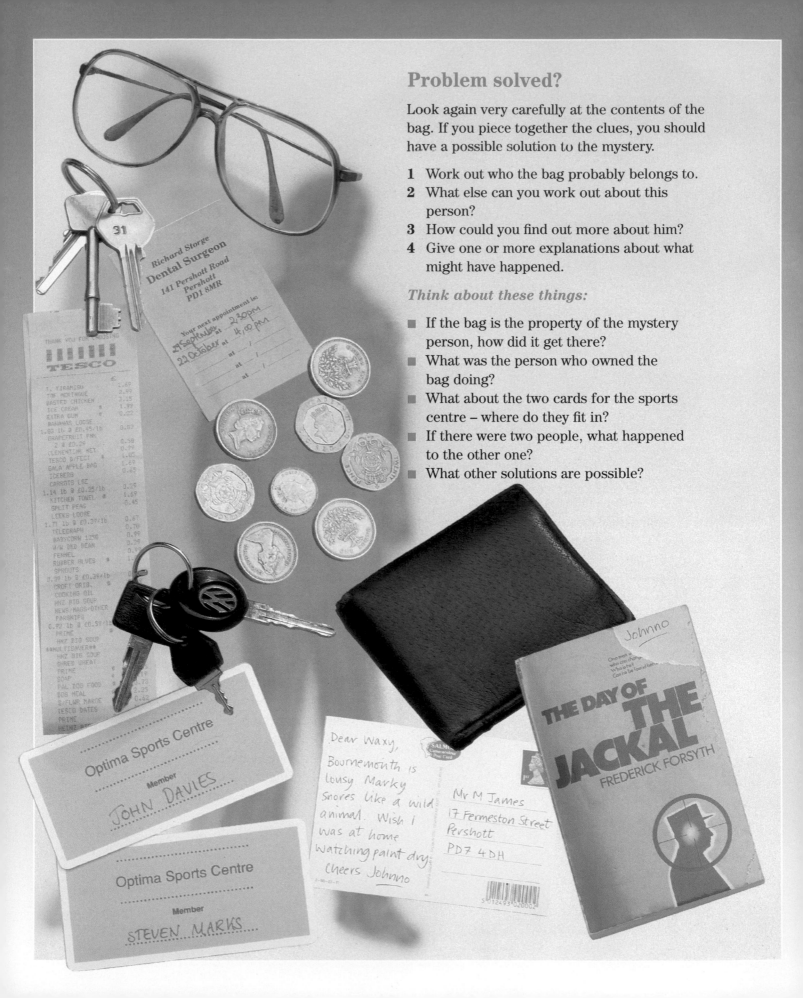

Problem solved?

Look again very carefully at the contents of the bag. If you piece together the clues, you should have a possible solution to the mystery.

1 Work out who the bag probably belongs to.
2 What else can you work out about this person?
3 How could you find out more about him?
4 Give one or more explanations about what might have happened.

Think about these things:

■ If the bag is the property of the mystery person, how did it get there?
■ What was the person who owned the bag doing?
■ What about the two cards for the sports centre – where do they fit in?
■ If there were two people, what happened to the other one?
■ What other solutions are possible?

Looking back at the mystery

Your teacher will tell you which of these assignments you need to complete.

1 Tell the story of all that has happened from the point of view of a pupil at Pershott High.

2 Imagine that a reporter interviews Robert Carson, the caretaker, on the morning he discovers the body. What does Robert Carson say?

3 Imagine that a reporter interviews Dr Nadia Sahir at Pershott General Hospital soon after the mystery man has been admitted. What does she say?

4 Imagine that a reporter interviews Mrs Sheila Buxton, the headteacher of Pershott High, once the identity of the man and what happened to him has been established. What does the head say?

5 Imagine you are the headteacher, Mrs Sheila Buxton. The governors ask you to send out a letter to parents about this incident. The purpose of the letter is to reassure parents about the school and to emphasise that Pershott High is a safe and secure place to be educated.

6 Prepare an article for the *Pershott Evening News* based on the events of the morning.

   ■ Look back carefully at pages 153 to 155.
   ■ Make as much as you can of the mystery of the case.
   ■ As well as the facts, you might include quotes from:
     – the police
     – Robert Carson, caretaker at Pershott High
     – Sheila Buxton, headteacher at Pershott High
     – Dr Nadia Sahir, doctor at Pershott General Hospital.
   ■ Remember to think especially about your headline.
     Choose one of the following headlines or make up a better one of your own:
     School Body Shock
     Mystery Man in Coma
     Who is This Man?

7 Prepare a follow-up article for the *Pershott Evening News* in which the full story of the mystery man is revealed.

   ■ This article would probably include quotes from the police and from the headteacher of the school.
   ■ It could also include some comment/explanation from a friend of the mystery man.
   ■ Once again the headline is important. Try out several possible headlines before choosing the one you think is best.

I dreamed I was flying

Page	Title	What you do	Why you do it
161	**I dreamed I was flying**	Look at a picture and answer some questions about it.	To start you thinking about the themes of the unit.
162–163	**Boy flying**	Read a poem, think about it and answer some questions about it.	To develop your ability to read poetry with imagination and intelligence.
164–167	**The death of Icarus**	Read a story and a poem about the same subject. Retell the story in different ways.	To develop your ability to read a story with imagination. To write for different audiences and purposes.
168–171	**Recklessly into the laps of the gods**	Read a newspaper story and look at the pictures that go with it. Think carefully about them and then write factually and imaginatively about the subject.	To develop your close reading and writing skills.
172	**What could he feel?**	Look back at the poem 'Boy flying' and study how the sentences in it were constructed.	To develop your understanding of how sentences work.
173	**The eagle**	Read a poem and think how to turn it into a video. Answer detailed questions about the poem.	To develop your ability to read in detail. To learn how to present information in different ways.
174	**Punctuation revision Wordpower**	Read a passage and use what you have learnt about punctuation to correct it. Look again at some of the words in the unit.	To revise what you have learnt about punctuation. To develop your vocabulary.

I dreamed I was flying

Just imagine...

It is **you** in the photograph.

- What can you see?
- What can you hear?
- What other sensations do you experience?
- What are your emotions?

Boy flying

Flying,
He saw the earth flat as a plate,
As if there were no hills, as if houses
Were only roofs, as if the trees
Were only the leaves that covered
The treetops. He could see the shadows
The clouds cast when they sailed over the fields,
He could see the river like the silver track
Left by a snail, and roads narrow as ribbons.

10   He could not see Mickey French next door,
In bed with a cold, nor his two sisters
Playing 'Happy Families' as they watched
The television. He could not see his kitten.

Flying,
He felt the air as solid as water
When he spread his fingers against it.
He felt it cool against his face, he felt
His hair whipped. He felt weightless
As if he were hollow, he felt the sun
20   Enormously bright and warm on his back,
He felt his eyes watering. He felt
The small, moist drops the clouds held.

He could not feel the grass, he could not
Feel the rough stones of the garden wall.
He could not remember the harsh, dry bark
Of the apple tree against his knees.

Flying,
He could hear the wind hissing, the note
Changed when he turned his head. He heard
His own voice when he sang. Very faintly,
He heard the school bus as it grumbled
Past the church, he thought he could hear
The voices of the people as they shouted
In amazement when they saw him swoop and glide.

He could not hear the birds sing, nor the chalk
Squeak against the blackboard, nor the mower
As it whirred along, nor the clock tick.
He could not hear the bacon sizzle in the pan,
He could not hear his friend calling him.

Leslie Norris

Thinking points

1 Think back to the ideas you had about flying when
   you looked at page 161. You thought about:
   ■ what you could see
   ■ what you could feel
   ■ what you could hear.
   How did your ideas compare with those of the poem?

2 Pick out two or three short sections in the poem that
   you think are striking. What do you like about them?

3 This poem follows a pattern. How would you describe
   the pattern?

4 Think about the poem as a whole. Think particularly
   about this contrast:

   He saw ...   *He could not see ...*
   He felt ...   *He could not feel ...*
   He heard ...   *He could not hear ...*

5 How would you describe the overall effect the poem
   has on you?

The death of Icarus

A Greek myth tells the story of Daedalus, a famous inventor. He designed the Labyrinth for Minos, King of Crete. Here the king kept a monster called the Minotaur, which was half man and half bull.

Minos later imprisoned Daedalus and his son Icarus on Crete. Daedalus racked his brains to think of a way of escaping with Icarus from their island prison.

Daedalus had an idea. He pretended to the guards that he had made a new kind of bow. Then he shot two large birds. He and Icarus made themselves wings from the large flight feathers of the birds. The only way they could fix the feathers to the framework was with wax. It was difficult to keep the work secret from the guards. Before long, however, all four wings were finished and they were ready to leave. They managed to smuggle
10 the wings up to the high terrace. They studied the birds soaring up above the palace. Before they chose their moment and leapt to join the birds, Daedalus warned young Icarus not to fly too close to the sun. He was afraid that as the day grew hot, the wax would melt and the wings would fall apart.

20 At first Icarus was terrified, but he soon found that flying was rather like swimming in deliciously warm water, without the tiresome business of getting wet. He was lighter than his father and as his confidence grew, he found he could swoop and soar and do aerobatics. With only an occasional glance over his shoulder, he had soon left his father far behind. The islands below him seemed quite large at first, but as he followed an eagle up towards the sun, they turned into tiny specks.

    Suddenly Icarus felt something tickling his left arm and then his right, his elbow and then his wrist. He couldn't scratch of
30 course, because of the wings, but he turned his head to look. To his horror he saw some of the feathers were beginning to trail across his arm as the wax began to melt and dribble away behind him. In his excitement he had flown too near the sun as it grew hotter and hotter towards midday. Suddenly, like a great bird that has been shot, he did a half-somersault and plunged with a long scream of 'Father!' deep into the sea.

    There was nothing his father could do as he flew over the place where his son had vanished in the brilliant blue of the sea. He flew on, resting occasionally on an island and at last he
40 reached Greece. However, he was still an outlaw, so eventually he found a ship that would take him to Sicily, and there he stayed, working again at his plans for new inventions and new buildings until he died of old age.

Elizabeth Seely

Icarus

Down through curling heat
from a still sea
the wax wings beat in dizzy fall,
melt into skewbald light then
trail white stars in a noon sky.

Judith Nicholls

Telling the tale

1 Report to Minos

Minos had ordered that Daedalus and Icarus should be carefully guarded, yet they escaped. You are one of the soldiers who were supposed to be guarding them. You saw what happened. You have to tell your Captain what you saw.

1 Read the story again.
2 Make a numbered list of the main things that you saw.
3 Think about how you feel as you tell the Captain your story.
4 Now write your version of the story.

TF

2 Picture book

You have been asked to write a picture book of Greek myths for young children. The story of Icarus is to take up two pages, with eight pictures and a short and simple retelling of the story.

1 Think about how you would divide up the story into eight sections. You may find it helps to give each section a short title, for example: *1. Daedalus has an idea.*
2 Decide what you would put in each of the pictures and write a clear description of each one.
3 Write the section of the story that goes with each picture.

3 Reference book

The extract on the right came from a reference book. It contains brief information about Greek history and myths for students of your age. You are going to write the entry for Icarus. You are only allowed 90 words.

1 Make sure that you know what this type of reference book is like. You may need to go to the library to do some research.
2 Make a list of the most important points in the story.
3 Write your version of the story as briefly as you can.
4 Count how many words you have used.
5 If you have used fewer than 90 words, check that you have not missed out anything important.
6 If you have used more than 90 words, you must cut and rewrite until your text is short enough.
7 Check that you have not missed out anything important.

Daedalus: famous Athenian inventor, designer of the **Labyrinth** where **Minos** King of Crete kept the **Minotaur**. Daedalus and his son **Icarus** were later imprisoned by

Recklessly into the laps

The latest daredevils
use kites to rocket into the sky
at six times the force of gravity.
James Kanter meets Britain's
record-breaking 'power-jumper'.

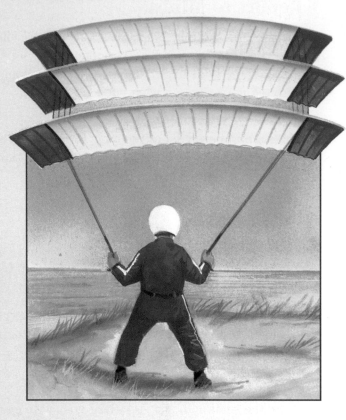

Kieron Chatterjea, 22, holds the Guinness World Record for 'power-jumping', a kind of wind-assisted human propulsion. Without explosives or fuel and using little more than a stack of three lilo-shaped kites, Kieron entered the history books last year by cannonballing himself a distance of 105ft [32 metres], the length of four London buses.

Power-jumping is so dangerous that most 'pilots' are loath to call it a sport, yet many continue to participate in formal competitions. Kieron broke his collarbone while developing power-jumping four years ago; a chairman of the American Kitefliers' Association shattered his pelvis in 1991; and a Dutchman fell 30ft [9 metres] to his death last year during an attempt to jump with kites while 'tethered' to the ground by a harness.

'If I had known how lunatic this was going to be, I would have never started it,' Kieron says. 'But as a pioneer, I feel I have a responsibility to make it safer for the other maniacs out there, who are bound to give it a go.'

The key to a safe launch is to have one leg

of the gods

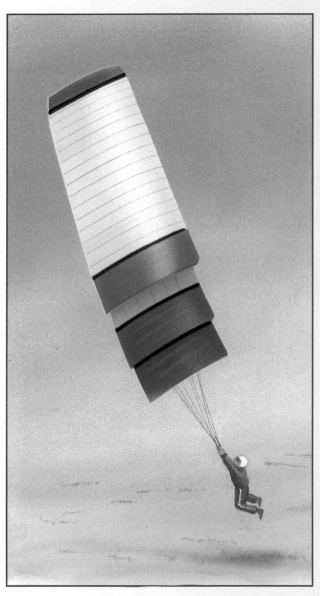

somersaults forwards into the air, legs above your head, and arms stretched to their limits by the massive acceleration.

Once you have reached about 25ft [7.7 metres], your body swings forward like a pendulum, until it is slowed by the canopy of kites over your head. The average touch-down occurs at about
40 20mph, but where you will land is never certain.

This enormous pull from the wind was first harnessed by the Flexifoil power kite, invented by two Englishmen 18 years ago. They saw it as the Formula One of the kite world, but intended that it be flown in the traditional way: with both feet firmly on the ground. Andrew Jones, co-developer and manufacturer of the Flexifoil, says: 'I think Kieron has been lucky not to get killed. Frankly, we try to keep low key about
50 the jumping phenomenon. But there are always going to be mad people who will do this kind of thing.'

The Independent

on the ground, the other locked against a post or ditch. Leaning back at 45 degrees, you should be able to bring the kites smoothly from the 'minimum power position', on one side of the wind, into the 'performance window' where
30 they surge upwards with explosive power.

Past this point, 'you're in the hands of the gods', says Kieron. Like it or not, your body

Hold the front page!

N'ICE ONE!

DROPPED IN IT!

STOP ME AND TRY ONE!

Keeping their cool

You are a new reporter for a popular tabloid daily paper. You have been given the job of writing an article about a power-jumping competition where this strange incident has happened. Choose one of the headlines on this page – or make up your own – and write your article.

Remember that your article should be short, and lively, but must tell the whole story.

What is power-jumping?

Words for the pictures

1 Read the article on pages 168–169.
2 Find the section that describes what happens
   in power-jumping.
3 Read it again and make sure that you understand it.
4 Look at the four pictures illustrating the article.
5 For each picture, write out the words from the
   article that describe what's happening:

   1) The key to a safe launch is to have one leg on the ground.

6 Now give each picture a title:

   The launch

7 Write a short caption (not more than 30 words)
   for each picture describing what it shows:

   The pilot keeps one foot on the ground.

How it works

Use the work you have done so far for these exercises.

1 Question and answer
Imagine that you have the opportunity to try power-
jumping for yourself (and that you have decided to
go ahead!). Make a list of ten questions that you would
like answered before your first 'flight'.

2 I don't understand!
You have been asked by a six-year-old what power-
jumping is. Write a simple explanation that s/he will
understand. Use the pictures on pages 168–169,
if you wish.

What could he feel?

Look again at the poem 'Boy flying' on pages 162–163. It is a 'list poem'; it lists the things that the boy could (and could not) see, feel and hear. You could set them out in a table like the one on the right:

subject	verb	
He	felt	the air
		his hair
		the sun
	could not feel	the grass

Make a table

- Look at the table again. It shows what the boy *felt*.
- Make similar tables for what he *saw* and *heard*.
- Look at what you have written. The things in the third column answer the question 'what?': for example, 'What could he feel?' This column contains the **objects** of the sentences.

Object

The object of a statement sentence comes after the verb and it refers to someone or something different from the subject. Look at the table on the right:

subject	verb	object
He	felt	the air
		his hair
		the sun

Make your own list poem

1 Choose one of these titles. Your poem can be about a boy or a girl:
 Girl flying
 Boy sleeping
 Girl swimming
 or make up a similar title of your own.
2 Make up three tables like those you have been working on, listing what s/he could and could not see, hear and feel. Think of as many objects as you can.
3 Now use your tables as the basis for your poem.

The eagle

He clasps the crag with crooked hands;
Close to the sun in lonely lands,
Ring'd with the azure world, he stands.

The wrinkled sea beneath him crawls;
He watches from his mountain walls,
And like a thunderbolt he falls.

Alfred, Lord Tennyson

Making the video

You have been asked to make a video about the
eagle. The sound track will be a reading of the
poem. What shot will you need for each group of
words?

1 Divide the poem into numbered sections.
2 Write out a 'shooting script' for your video like
   this:

Section	Text	Shot
1	He clasps...hands	Close-up of eagle's talons on rock.

Reading in detail EXT

This is only a short poem, but the more closely you look at it, the more
you realise just how closely Tennyson has looked at the eagle.

1 Compare the first line with this alternative:
   It grips the crag with crooked claws
   What is the effect of using:
   a 'He' rather than 'It'?
   b 'hands' rather than 'claws'?
   c 'clasps' rather than 'grips'?
2 The eagle is literally 'closer' to the sun than
   the creatures below, but do the words 'close
   to the sun' suggest anything else?

3 'Azure' means 'sky-blue'. What picture do
   you see when you read line 3?
4 Why is the sea 'wrinkled', and why does it
   'crawl'? What does line 4 add to our image
   of the eagle?
5 What picture does the last line of the poem
   give you?
6 Write a few sentences summing up your
   thoughts and feelings about the poem.

Punctuation revision

Copy out the passage adding all the necessary punctuation.

the hunt had ranged far and the young king full of exhilaration for the wind streaming past his face and the bunched power of the stallion pulsing beneath him had far outstripped the rest of his knights only king bors of gaunes riding a fiery french charger from his own country had been able to keep him in sight and now he came up with arthur as the king reined in his horse and looked about him they had gone deep into the forest and they stood in a little clearing where the air struck curiously chill and damp and the horses breath plumed upwards like smoke in the clear air they could not hear the hounds they could not hear the huntsmans horn it was as if they had stumbled into another world my lord said bors slowly i do not like this place they heard a rustle in the bushes and turned to see a richly-dressed dwarf standing before them borss horse laid back its ears and whinnied what are you said bors what do you want with the king the dwarf said nothing but bowed low with a courtly flourish then solemnly motioned arthur and bors to follow him bors looked doubtful but arthur dismounted at once lead on friend he said well follow you

Wordpower

All these words are in the unit you have been reading.

1 Explain the meanings of as many as you can.
2 For those you cannot explain, find them in the unit
    and try to work out their meaning from the sentence
    they are in. Then check them in a dictionary.
3 If there are any left, look them up in the dictionary.
4 Make sure that you can spell them.

word	page	line	word	page	line	word	page	line
weightless	162	18	aerobatics	165	24	skewbald	166	4
amazement	163	34	propulsion	168	3	pelvis	168	15
terrace	164	10	participate	168	11	pendulum	169	37
delicious(ly)	165	21	tether(ed)	168	17	canopy	169	38
confidence	165	23	minimum	169	28	phenomenon	169	50
occasional(ly)	165	39	acceleration	169	35			

Mission to Zureon

The Euro Space Minister announced today that the first mission to set up a colony on another planet will blast off into the unknown early next year. Each of the countries in the United European Community will select fifteen brave explorers to take this first step into the unknown and set up a space colony on the planet Zureon.

Zureon has been chosen because it is the nearest planet containing sufficient water to support human life. Nevertheless, the planet has many dangers, and those who go on the mission will require many different strengths. Final details about the mission will be announced at a Press Conference shortly before blast-off. Stay tuned to this channel.

Action: Read text.

Animate graphic.

Absorb ideas.

More: Pages 175 thru' 182

Competition to join the expedition is likely to be fierce, even though it is unlikely that the expedition members will ever be able to return to Earth. The planet Zureon is over 30 light years away from Earth at the closest point of its orbit around the galaxy.

The Minister stated that citizens from all the countries in the Community could apply to join this exciting leap forward into the 22nd century. However, applicants must be aged between 18 and 30, and have a high standard of fitness and health to withstand the hardships of the journey.

All those wishing to join the interstellar ship *Galactic Voyager* when she blasts off from the Space Centre at Milton Keynes should key in significant life details and an application videotext without delay. Selection interviews will be held during the next month, and fifteen lucky pioneers will be chosen to start training for the expedition.

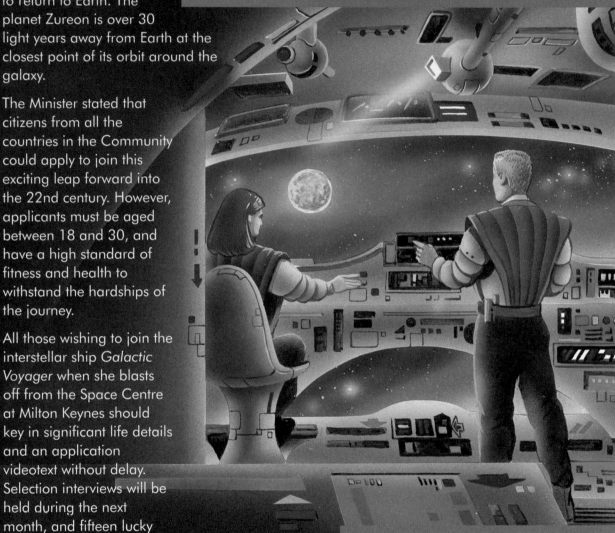

Action Read text.
        Animate graphic.
        Absorb ideas.
More Pages 176 thru' 182

Toni Beardsley, leading scorer for European Champions Everpool last season, dropped a bombshell at the club today when she said that she wanted to go on the mission to Zureon. 'It's something I've always dreamed of doing,' she said. 'I've had two great seasons at this club, but you have to take your chances when they are there!' Apart from being a superb player, Toni also has a degree in astro-physics which gives her a great chance of making the trip. 'Football and astro-physics are pretty much the same thing really. They're both to do with calculating the flight of a moving sphere through time and space. Maybe that's how I manage to get on the end of so many crosses!'

Officials at the club made no comment about the news, but it is obvious that they would be unhappy to lose the talented striker who broke the Euroleague transfer record when she signed for the club. Since being with Everpool, Toni has won two Eurochampions medals, and scored the winning goal in last season's Intercontinental Cup. In an exclusive interview given only to Holovision Sport, Toni revealed the heartache it had taken her to make up her mind.

'It wasn't an easy decision to make. But I'm 22 now, and probably only have a couple of seasons left at the top. This opportunity was just too good to miss. You've got to admit too that the world's in a bit of a mess at the moment. There's the radiation desert after the accident in 2032 and all the mutations that caused.

Screen 3 of 8
Status Interactive
Text Videoprint
Subject Soccer Ace applies for Zureon Mission

I mean, my great grandfather said he played on grass, not purple plastic. And with the population explosion, there's just not enough room in the world to breathe. That's in those places where the air is still fit to breathe. I've come off the pitch sometimes nearly choking to death from pollution. I like the idea of starting off in a new world with plenty of room, trying to avoid the mistakes we've made on this planet. That's why I hope I'm picked for the team.'

Toni has already filled in her application videotext, and is hoping to be selected for interview. Why don't you join her?

Latest: SENSATION! Robot-wrestler took bribes. Fights fixed claims ex-manager. See Screen 95 / 207 for full report.

Action Read text.
Absorb ideas.
More Pages 177 thru' 182

Screen 4 of 8

Status Interactive

Text Videoprint

Subject How to Apply for Zureon Mission

TF

If you have the courage, the skills, and the physical make-up to join the expedition, here's how to apply.

1 Prepare a CV which gives the following information:

Name
Age
Identity No.
Sex
Address
Genetic type (human / android / alien)
Nationality (include planet of birth)
Credit rating
Security rating
Intelligence rating
Health record (include transplants, or robotic implants)
Occupation
Qualifications
Previous relevant experience

2 Produce a video print text which explains why you believe you might be a suitable member of the mission. Download this to Channel 94 soonest.

3 Take part in the interviews to select the fifteen British members of the expedition. Volunteers are needed to interview the applicants; in your application text state whether you wish to be a member of the interviewing panel.

4 Complete the Initiative Tests. Details on next screens.

The names of the lucky winners selected to take part in this historic mission will be announced at the Press Conference before take-off.

Action Prepare CV.

Produce application text.

Take part in selection interview.

Take test.

More Pages 178 thru' 182

Zureon lies beyond our solar system towards the outer regions of the galaxy at a distance of some 35 light years away. There are two poles and seven distinct zones on the planet. Further data about the planet follows.

One of the first decisions the expedition leaders will have to make is where to set up the base colony on the planet. Remember that the base will be inhabited by human, alien and android life forms. The choice of site must take account of this. Show that you have the necessary decision-making skills to join the expedition by choosing the best site for the space base. Applicants are encouraged to discuss this as a group in order to reach the best decision. Include an explanation for your choice with your application.

Zureon mission database – facts

Duration of voyage	37.5 light years at sub-light speed.
Crew status	In hibersleep, body temperatures lowered to −50°C to reduce aging processes.
Approach to planet	Orange alert. Establish orbit, shuttle craft to be sent to surface.
Landing area	Unknown, verify soonest.
Planet mass	63% Earthmass. Gravitational field decreased.
Atmosphere	48% Earthozone. Respirators required initially, oxygen levels to be raised by introduction of plant-life.
Water	90% Earthvolume. Choice of planet for colony dependent upon large natural deposits of H_2O.
Temperature range	Extreme. From -1500°C to +1800°C.
Life forms	None detected with life status. Evidence of previous extinct life-forms. Advise caution. Next–

Action: Reach decision.

Select site for space base.

More: Pages 179 thru' 182

The planet maintains a regular orbit around its sun-star, Ignis. The orbit lasts for 163 earth years; this is the length of the Zureon 'year'. At its closest point to Ignis, it is likely that the temperature on the planet will increase considerably. How this will affect water supplies on the planet is unknown. The colonists must be prepared for all changes in climate.

Action: **Rotate planet using interactive video.**

Identify poles and zones using key.

More: **Pages 180 thru' 182**

Planet has two poles with extremes of temperature. Remainder of planet surface divided into seven zones.

A Volcano Zone ▷ Highly dangerous: many active volcanoes. Ground between flat. Ash from the volcanoes makes excellent fertiliser. Air poor. Hot thermal rivers are source of power and water.

B Earthquake Zone ▷ Frequent earthquakes cause deep chasms. Rocks glow red hot and explode. Could provide geo-thermal energy. Water, air and solar power. Mining possible. Climate very favourable.

C Desert Zone ▷ The closest region to Ignis, nearest star to planet. Hottest zone on planet, with rich supplies of solar energy. Little water, high temperatures, violent dust storms. Underground caves could provide some protection. Rich in metal ores.

D Ice Pole ▷ Coldest region on planet. Contains most of the water. Little sun available for solar power, but air does contain oxygen. Climate poor, frequent snowstorms and blizzards.

E Twin Moons ▷ Aggron and Heros. No atmosphere or water. Solar energy available. Long-term inhabitation unlikely, but possible first stage base.

F Radiation Zone ▷ Very radioactive due to large deposits of uranium. A useful source of nuclear power, but protection would be needed. Plants difficult to grow, though mutant crops would grow to enormous sizes. Air unbreathable, water contaminated.

G Swamp Zone ▷ Evil-smelling swamps have simple plant life. Almost no solid ground. Green slime covers everything. Abundant water, rich in oxygen. Crops would grow quickly if swamps drained. Climate hot, steamy.

H Mountain Zone ▷ Mountains rise to 48,000 metres, rocky and sheer. Avalanches dangerous. Transport problems. Water plentiful. Valleys protected against harsh climate, air plentiful. Plant life likely to grow abundantly.

I Acid Seas ▷ Vast oceans of very dangerous acid. Air poisonous due to gases. Islands are rich in mineral crystals for making solar panels. Acid can be used to generate electricity and distill water.

J Meteorite Zone ▷ Many meteorite strikes. Many craters, some very deep. Meteorite showers every ten to fifteen years. Water, air and solar power abundant. Rich in metals from meteorites.

Action: Read text.

Absorb information.

More: Page 182

Produce a design, either as a plan or as a drawing, that shows how the space base, which will provide the first, permanent foothold on the planet, should be constructed.

You will need to consider:

≡ The shape of the base.
≡ The materials from which it is to be constructed. Applicants should describe the strengths and properties of any new materials used in their design.
≡ The method used to assemble it. (Remember that this needs to be done quickly.)
≡ The ways in which it protects the colonists from heat/cold, radiation, meteorites.
≡ The layout of the base, including these facilities:
Spaceport
Vehicle bay and workshops
Living and leisure quarters
Sleeping accommodation
Cooking facilities
Washing facilities
Laboratories
Greenhouses
Medical centre
Life-support system
Power system.

All plans and designs should be ready for display at the final Press Conference when the winning design will be chosen.

Good luck to all applicants.

Action: Reach decision.

Design space base.

Take part in Press Conference.

Today is an important date in the history of peoplekind. For the first time, human beings are reaching out to begin life on another planet.

The voyage from Earth has passed without significant event. All systems have functioned successfully. The gyrocomputer has guided us into orbit around the planet Zureon. From my observation window I can see it faintly glowing below, illuminated by the light of the star that is its sun, its twin moons shining above the horizon. It is a new, unexplored world. A new life beckons.

The crew have been aroused from hibersleep by the android crew which have brought us here. Health status data for each crew member is being computed. Awakening after 35 years' sleep is a strange experience, like being reborn. I am rediscovering the use of my limbs, everything seems new to my senses. There is an air of excitement throughout the whole ship.

One problem has arisen. The shuttle party left for the planet surface four earth hours ago. They were to collect data from each of the planet zones. But while exploring the Desert Zone, they have discovered evidence of intelligent life on the planet: a strange hieroglyph burned by laser into the rock itself. Our language experts have begun to decipher its strange message.

The safety of the crew depends upon them understanding its message. I need to know how this language works, and what this message means.

So far our experts have unlocked the following clues.

 The star, the sun

 The arachnid-alien

 To live, insect aliens live

 The dwelling, house

 The insect-alien

 The planet surface, the ground

 The alien planet

 The planet Zureon

 The moon

 To burn, to get hot

 The tools

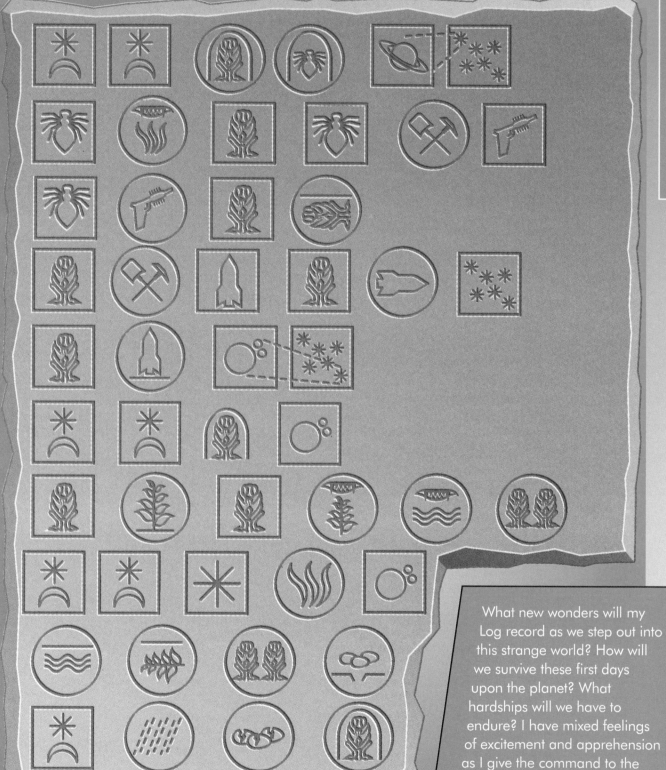

What new wonders will my Log record as we step out into this strange world? How will we survive these first days upon the planet? What hardships will we have to endure? I have mixed feelings of excitement and apprehension as I give the command to the construction parties to begin work on the space base. What does this message mean?

What on Zureon will happen to us...?

Guide to language

Grammar

Grammar describes how language works:

- how words are arranged to make sentences
- the ways in which some words change to fit into sentences.

It is useful to be able to talk about how sentences work. It can help you to overcome problems you meet when reading and writing. It enables you to talk to other people (eg your teacher) about your writing.

Sentences

There are four different kinds of sentence. Each one is used for a different purpose. Each follows a different pattern.

Statement

> *I like music.*

Question

There are three types of question:

Yes/no questions

> *Do you like music?*

Wh- questions

> *What kind of music do you like?*

Either/or questions

> *Do you like rock or classical?*

There is more about this on page 149.

Directive

> *Play that music!*

Directives can have many different purposes, for example: to command, to request, to warn, and to advise.

There is more about directives on page 135.

Exclamation:

> *What a great song that is!*

Parts of a sentence

Every full statement sentence contains a subject and a verb. Many sentences contain other parts after the verb. The parts of a sentence may be a single word, or a group of words, a phrase.

Subject

The subject of a statement sentence comes at the beginning of the sentence and often tells us what or who the sentence will be about:

> **My friend Alison Greenaway** *won the race.*

Verb

In a statement sentence the verb comes after the subject.

> *My friend Alison Greenaway* **won** *the race.*

The subject of the sentence can be singular or plural. The verb must agree with the subject:

> *Alison* **likes** *athletics.*
> *My sister and I* **like** *netball.*

When we are writing or speaking, the events we describe can take place in the past, the present or the future. We can show this in two ways:

- by using time words like *yesterday, next week*
- by the tense of the verb (I *like*/I *liked*).

There is more about time and tense on pages 78 and 109.

The verb in a sentence may consist of one word, or a group of words, a verb phrase. In a verb phrase, there will be a full verb and one or more auxiliary verbs.

This is explained on pages 56 and 57.

Object

As well as a subject and a verb, many sentences contain an object. This comes after the verb in a statement sentence and it refers to a different person or thing from the subject:

> *Alison likes* **athletics**.

There is more about objects on page 172.

Words

The words we use to build sentences can be grouped into different classes according to the way in which they are used. It is useful to know the names of these classes so that you can use them when you are talking about your own writing and other people's.

Nouns

Nouns are words that refer to people, places, things and ideas. They answer the questions 'What?' or 'Who?' Most nouns will fit into one or more of the blanks in these sentences:

> *This is a _____ .*
> *I like _____ .*
> *Have you got any _____ ?*

Nouns can be formed from verbs, adjectives, and other nouns, by adding a suffix, like **-er, -ness, -ment, -ity**.

There is more about this on page 10.

Pronouns

Pronouns stand in place of nouns, or groups of words doing the same work as nouns. We use them to avoid having to repeat the same noun over and over again. The personal pronouns are:

I	me
you	you
he/she/it	him/her/it
we	us
they	them

Adjectives

Adjectives are words that help to make nouns more precise. They answer the question, 'What kind of ... ?'
Adjectives are used in two main ways:

- with a noun: ***My red** car.*
- after verbs like 'is': *My car is **red**.*

Adjectives can be used to compare two or more things:

> *Angela is **taller** than Jamie.*
> *Peter is the **tallest** person in our class.*

We can also alter the meaning of an adjective by putting words before it:

> *Peter is **very** tall.*

There is more about this on page 34.

Verbs

As we have seen above, every full statement sentence contains a verb. The verb in a sentence can be one word or a number of words (called a verb phrase). If the verb in a sentence is made up of several words, these are all called verbs. Confusing, but that's the way it is.

There is more about this on page 56.

Adverbs

Adverbs work with verbs and answer questions like 'How?' 'When?' and 'Where?'

> He left **quickly.**
> He jumped **back.**
> They returned **later.**

They are also used with adjectives and other adverbs (and then they answer the question 'How much?')

> He left **very** quickly.

Adverbs can be formed from adjectives, by adding the suffix **-ly**:

> quickly, happily

There is more about adverbs on page 99.

Parts of a word

Words can be built up from different parts.

Stem

Every word has a stem and many words consist of this alone:

> happy   fortune

Prefix

A section that is added before the stem is called a prefix. Prefixes are used to change the meaning of a stem:

> **un**happy

Suffix

A section that is added after the stem is called a suffix. Suffixes are used to change the class of a word. For example a noun can be changed into an adjective:

> fortun**ate**

Punctuation

We use punctuation marks to make our writing clear and easy to read. If you punctuate badly – or not at all – people will find it very difficult to understand your writing.

Full stops

The main use of a full stop is to mark the end of a sentence. One of the commonest mistakes people make is to forget to do this, so it is always a good idea to check, when you have finished writing, to make sure that you have put in all the full stops.

Full stops are also used in abbreviations:

- to show that a single letter stands for a word:
  H. Ponsonby for Herbert Ponsonby
  S. for south

- to show that a group of letters stands for a word:
  Capt. for Captain

There are some exceptions to these rules:

- Abbreviations made up only of capital letters (BBC, IRA) are often written without full stops
- Mr, Mrs, Ms are usually written without full stops.

Capital letters

Capital letters are used for:

- the first letter in a sentence
- for the pronoun I
- the first letters of names of people, places
- the first letters of people's titles (Mr, Lady)
- the first letters of names of titles of books, films and television/radio programmes (usually it is only the main words that have capital letters)
- abbreviations, when a single letter stands for a word
- for emphasis – for example, in advertisements.

There is more about capital letters on page 16.

Commas

A comma is used to mark a pause or short break in a sentence. One common use for it is to separate things in a list.

This is explained on page 72.

Commas are also used to put things 'in brackets':

Mr Carter's boss, **John Thompson***, thought the car was legally parked.*

This is explained more fully on page 107.

Colons

Colons are used:

- to introduce a list
- before a piece of speech, instead of a comma.

There are examples of this on page 143.

Semi-colons

This marks a stronger pause or break than a comma. It is also sometimes used to separate things in a list.

This is explained on page 143.

Apostrophes

There are two uses for the apostrophe:

To show when one or more letters have been missed out:

I have not → *I haven't*

To show that something belongs to someone:

The book belonging to Mary → *Mary's book*
The car belonging to my parents → *my parents' car*

There is more about apostrophes on page 128.

Setting out a script

There are a number of different ways of doing this.

They are explained in detail on page 98.

Punctuating direct speech

The rules for direct speech are explained on page 39.

Spelling

There is no simple way to become a good speller. Some people seem to find it easier than others. You can do something about it, however:

- Keep a spelling list (in the back of your English book, or in a separate notebook). Make sure that you write down the correct spelling of words you find difficult. Keep it in alphabetical order, or you will never be able to find the word you want.
- If there is a word you repeatedly get wrong, do this:

Look	at the word correctly spelled.
Cover	it up.
Write	it on a piece of paper.
Check	that you have got it right.

- If you are not sure which of two spellings is right, try writing them both out to see which one looks right.
- Use a dictionary to check your spelling.
- Above all, **read** as much as possible.

Common rules

Making plurals with 's'

- Usually, just add **s** .... books, ices
- Words that end in **s, x, ch, sh,** add **es** .... masses, taxes, branches, rushes
- Words that end in **y**
  if the letter before the **y** is a vowel, add **s** .... days
  if the letter before the **y** is a consonant,
  cut off the **y** and add **ies** .... babies
- Words that end in **f** or **fe**,
  change the **f/fe** to **ves** .... wolves
  Exceptions .... roofs, dwarfs, beliefs, chiefs, proofs
- Words that end in **o**, usually just add **s** .... pianos
  Exceptions .... tomatoes, potatoes, volcanoes, heroes

Adding -ing and -ed

Usually, you just add **ing** or **ed**, but there are some important special rules.

- words ending in **consonant + y**: .... try
  change the **y** to **i** before adding **ed** .... tried
- words of one syllable, with a
  long vowel ending in **e**: .... fade
  remove the **e** and add the ending .... faded fading
- words of one syllable, with a short
  vowel and ending in a single consonant: .... fit
  double the consonant and add the ending .... fitted fitting

ie or ei?

For words in which these letters make a long **ee** sound use:

i before **e** .... thief

except after **c** .... receive

Exceptions .... seize weir weird

-able/-ible

The rules for this are on page 40.

-ant/-ent, -ance/-ence

■ Words ending in **-ant/-ent** are usually adjectives.

■ If a word can be spelled either way, the **-ant** version is a noun and the **-ent** version is an adjective: independant (n) independent (adj)

■ If the adjective is spelled **-ant**, then the noun is spelled **-ance**: *important/importance* (and the same for **-ent/-ence**).

■ If the suffix is preceded by a **t** or a **v**, then it is usually **-ant/-ance**.

There is an exercise on this on page 100.